BLACK & DECKER ®
HOME IMPROVEMENT LIBRARY™

Built-In Projects
for the Home

CREATIVE
PUBLISHING
international

MINNETONKA, MINNESOTA

www.howtobookstore.com

Contents

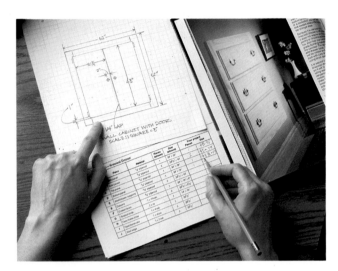

Copyright © 1993
Creative Publishing international, Inc.
5900 Green Oak Drive
Minnetonka, Minnesota 55343
1-800-328-3895
www.howtobookstore.com
All rights reserved
Printed in U.S.A.

Books available in this series:
New Everyday Home Repairs, Carpentry: Tools • Shelves • Walls • Doors, Building Decks, Home Plumbing Projects & Repairs, Basic Wiring & Electrical Repairs, Workshop Tips & Techniques, Advanced Home Wiring, Carpentry: Remodeling, Landscape Design & Construction, Bathroom Remodeling, Built-in Projects for the Home, Refinishing & Finishing Wood, Exterior Home Repairs & Improvements, Home Masonry Repairs & Projects, Building Porches & Patios, Flooring Projects & Techniques, Advanced Deck Building, Advanced Home Plumbing, Remodeling Kitchens, Finishing Basements & Attics, Stonework & Masonry Projects

Library of Congress
Cataloging-in-Publication Data

Built-in projects for the home.

p. cm.—(Black & Decker home improvement library)
Includes index.
ISBN 0-86573-730-4 (hardcover).
ISBN 0-86573-731-2 (softcover).
1. Built-in furniture.
I. Cy DeCosse Incorporated.
II. Series.
TT197.5.B8B85 1993
684.1'6—dc20   93-8783

President/CEO: Michael Eleftheriou
VP/Retail Sales & Marketing: Kevin Haas
VP/Retail Publishing: Linda Ball

Executive Editor: Bryan Trandem
Creative Editor: Tim Himsel
Managing Editor: Michelle Skudlarek
Editorial Director: Jerri Farris

BUILT-IN PROJECTS FOR THE HOME
Created by: The Editors of Creative Publishing international, Inc., in cooperation with Black & Decker. BLACK&DECKER. is a trademark of the Black & Decker Corporation and is used under license.

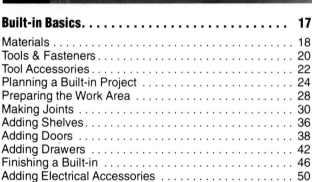

Project Director: Paul Currie
Project Manager: Carol Harvatin
Senior Editor: Bryan Trandem
Editors: Mark Johanson, Anne Price
Art Director: Dave Schelitzche
Senior Art Director: Tim Himsel
Technical Production Editor: Jim Huntley
Assistant Technical Production Editor:
  Gary Sandin
Vice President Planning & Production:
  Jim Bindas
Copy Editor: Janice Cauley
Contributing Editor: Dick Sternberg
Shop Supervisor: Phil Juntti
Set Builders: John Nadeau, Mike Peterson,
  Greg Wallace
Production Manager: Amelia Merz

Production Staff: Adam Esco, Joe Fahey,
  Mike Hehner, Jeff Hickman, Robert
  Powers, Mike Schauer, Julie Sutphen, Kay
  Wethern, Nik Wogstad
Photo Studio Manager: Mike Parker
Creative Photo Coordinator:
  Cathleen Shannon
Assistant Studio Managers: Marcia
  Chambers, Rena Tassone
Lead Photographer: Mark Macemon
Photographers: Rebecca Hawthorne,
  Rex Irmen, William Lindner, Paul Najlis,
  Chuck Nields, Mike Parker
Technical Illustrations: Kiehne Graphics
Styling Director: Bobbette Destiche
Photo Stylists: Deanna Despard, Coralie
  Sathre, Joanne Wawra
Contributing Photographers: Kim Bailey,
  Doug Deutcher, Paul Markerte
Model: Paul Toft

Contributing Manufacturers: Cooper
  Industries; Honeywell Corporation;
  Northern States Power Company; Waxman
  Industries, Inc.

Printed on American paper by:
  R. R. Donnelley & Sons Co.
1 0 9 8 7 6

Introduction

Built-in storage cabinets, shelves, and activity centers give your home a unique, custom-crafted look. Joined permanently to the structure of the house, built-ins change the look and layout of your home at a fraction of the cost of a major remodeling job.

Custom-made built-ins serve many of the same functions as the ready-made cabinets and storage units available at furniture stores and home centers. In addition to providing storage, built-ins made from quality materials add decorative interest to a room. But unlike ready-made products that are mass-produced, do-it-yourself built-ins create a unique look. The cost of materials for making built-ins is much less than the cost of ready-made furniture.

Built-ins are ideally suited for rooms with odd shapes or sizes, or for awkward, wasted spaces where standard furniture is not practical. A dim, cavernous space under a basement stairway can become a bright snack center for a recreation room. Empty knee-wall space under a sloped roof line can hold spacious dresser drawers. A long, narrow room can be divided into two separate living areas by adding an open-sided room divider.

Built-in Projects for the Home opens with a preview of the ten how-to projects featured in the book, with ideas for adapting each project to different uses.

Then, a section on built-in basics introduces you to the materials, tools, and skills needed to plan, build, and finish any of the featured projects in the book. Detailed planning information shows you how to adapt a featured built-in to fit your own needs. As you construct your built-ins, turn to this reference section whenever you need more information on the techniques shown.

Finally, you'll find complete how-to directions for constructing ten different built-in projects, rang-

ing from simple recessed shelves to an elaborate full-wall entertainment center. Chosen for their versatility, these project designs can be adapted easily for different building materials or to unique space requirements. With each built-in you have the option of completing the project exactly as shown or adapting it to meet your needs. And all projects can be built using everyday hand and power tools, and ordinary materials available at any home center.

Well-designed built-ins create permanent, organized storage by making clever use of existing spaces. They make a house seem larger, redefine how a room is used, and turn an ordinary house into a one-of-a-kind home you will be proud to own and show.

Project Preview

As you will see on the following pages, built-in projects provide useful storage while giving your home unique visual appeal. The featured projects range from simple wall cabinets to large built-ins that define the look and feel of an entire room. Some can be built in a few hours, while others may require a long weekend.

Each project can be built using a wide variety of materials, and the designs themselves were created so they can be adapted easily to fit unique spaces or special uses. Project variations are limited only by your creativity.

Built-ins become permanent features of your home, so plan carefully to ensure that your projects make efficient use of space and adequately meet the needs of your life-style. When choosing a location for a built-in, look for wall or floor spaces with unusual sizes or shapes, or areas that see little day-to-day use. By taking advantage of wasted space, a well-planned built-in can make a room seem larger. Built-ins that are recessed into wall spaces are especially effective because they add organized storage areas without using up valuable floor space.

A well-planned built-in project uses design details and building materials that complement the overall look of your home. Always try to make your project look like it was part of the original home plan—not an afterthought. Built-ins that are well designed and carefully constructed make your home more useful for you, more attractive to visitors, and more appealing to potential buyers.

Entertainment center (pages 116 to 125) organizes and stores bulky electronic equipment. It has a hardwood face frame, with cabinet doors and drawers that hide the equipment when it is not in use. This entertainment center features a modular center unit and two end units that are built separately. The overall width of the entertainment center, as shown, is 6 ft., 8". The project can be adapted easily by building additional end units.

6

Project Preview

Kneewall cabinet (pages 58 to 63) makes productive use of the low wall space found under a slanted roof line. For more extensive storage, position several cabinets side-by-side. **A:** Make an efficient, simple entertainment center by fitting the kneewall cabinet with shelves, cabinet doors, and electrical receptacles. **B:** Create space-saving storage shelves for toys, games, or books. **C:** Make a clothes dresser by adding drawers to the knee-wall cabinet.

Recessed wall shelves (pages 54 to 57) fit inside the space between wall studs. **A:** Create a small game or storage cabinet by adding doors. **B:** Create a pass-through between rooms by opening the wall from both sides and installing a wide shelf. **C:** Make a decorative display by adding several open shelves.

9

Project Preview

Floor-to-ceiling shelves (pages 68 to 73) are constructed with stationary middle shelves for strength, and adjustable shelves for flexible storage. **A:** Create a home library in any room by covering a wall with floor-to-ceiling shelves. **B:** Highlight decorative collectibles by adding low-voltage light fixtures (page 50) to the bottom sides of shelves.

Platform bench (pages 74 to 81) is a unique built-in with old-style charm. **A:** Make an indoor potting surface for plants by topping the bench with water-resistant ceramic tile. Keep planting supplies inside the bench. **B:** Create open storage for keeping quilts, decorative items, or oversized books. **C:** Build a traditional window seat by adding seat cushions and cabinet doors.

Project Preview

Basic wall cabinet and base cabinet (pages 88 to 97) feature a simple, universal design used by professional cabinet-makers. Basic cabinets can be adapted to a variety of uses, and work well in almost any room. **A:** Create utility cabinets for a laundry room, basement, or garage by building basic cabinets using inexpensive pine face frames and plywood panels. Finish the cabinets with enamel paint. **B:** Make a decorative hutch for a dining room or living room by building the cabinets from quality hardwood materials, and installing custom-made glass doors.

Corner cabinet (pages 82 to 87) provides ample storage by making good use of empty corner space. **A:** Add a unique bedroom wardrobe by building the corner cabinet with extra shelves and cabinet doors. **B:** Make a computer work center by equipping the corner cabinet with electrical receptacles and low-voltage lights.

Room divider (pages 106 to 115) separates a room into two living areas. **A:** Make an informal dining area by building a room divider next to the kitchen area and installing a wide countertop to provide an eating surface. **B:** Create a home study by using a room divider to isolate a small portion of a room.

A

B

Project Preview

Understairs work center (pages 98 to 105) makes use of the triangular space underneath a stairway—an area that is wasted space in most homes. **A:** Make a space-saving home office with a wide desktop and plenty of storage for supplies. **B:** Create a snack center for a recreation room by adding a ceramic countertop, a microwave oven, and a small refrigerator.

Utility shelving (pages 64 to 67) is a simple built-in that provides versatile storage for any unfinished space or informal living area. **A:** Store recycling containers and oversized lawn and garden supplies in a garage or shed. **B:** Raise workshop tools and camping equipment away from damp basement floors. **C:** Dress up utility shelves for family room storage by adding side panels and a face frame. Face frame pieces can be unscrewed and removed to rearrange shelves.

Built-In Basics

Materials

Built-in projects can vary considerably in size and style, but most can be constructed with materials available at any home improvement center. In some cases, you may need to visit a woodworker's supply store or large wholesale lumber yard to find unique woods, unusual moldings, or specialty hardware items.

To save money, construct your built-ins using finish-grade plywood for the main body (carcass), then trim exposed areas with more costly solid woods and moldings.

Lumber: Redwood (A) and cedar (B) are warm-colored softwoods used for exposed surfaces of a built-in. Because of their attractive color and grain, they usually are left unfinished or coated with a clear finish. Pine (C) is an easy-to-cut softwood often used for built-ins that will be painted. Framing lumber (D) includes rough grades of softwood pine and fir. It is used for structural framing and utility shelving. Poplar (E), a light-colored hardwood with very straight grain, is an excellent wood for fine painted surfaces. Maple (F) and oak (G) are heavy, strong hardwoods with attractive grain patterns. They usually are finished with tinted oils or stains.

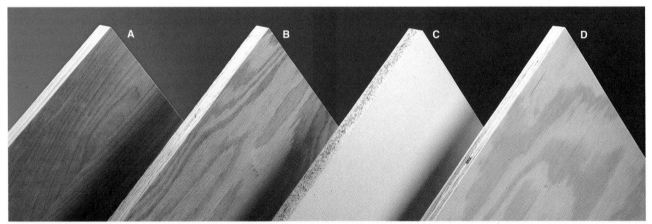

Sheet goods: Finish-grade plywood, including birch plywood (A) and oak plywood (B) are made from several layers of softwood veneer sandwiched between hardwood surface veneers. Finish-grade plywoods are used for exposed areas of a built-in, and usually are edged with hardwood strips or moldings. Birch plywood frequently is used for surfaces that will be painted, and oak plywood is usually finished with tinted oils or stains. Particleboard (C), coated with a plastic resin called melamine, is used for making contemporary-style built-ins. Sanded pine plywood (D) is a good material for built-ins that will be painted, or for hidden areas. **NOTE:** Most sheet goods are sold in 4 ft. × 8 ft. sheets, in 1/4", 1/2", or 3/4" thicknesses; some types also are sold in 2 ft. × 4 ft. and 4 ft. × 4 ft. sheets.

Trim moldings are both decorative and functional. They can be used to cover gaps around the base and sides of a built-in, to hide the edges of plywood surfaces, or simply to add visual interest to the project. Moldings are available in dozens of styles, but the samples shown here are widely available at all home improvement centers.

Synthetic trim moldings, available in many styles, are less expensive than hardwood moldings. Synthetic moldings are made of wood composites (A) or rigid foam (B) covered with a layer of melamine.

Baseboard molding (C) is used to trim the bottom edge of a built-in along the floor line. Choosing molding that matches the baseboard used elsewhere in your home gives your project a natural, built-in look.

Hardwood strips (D) are used to construct face frames for a built-in, and to cover unfinished edges of plywood shelves. Maple, oak, and poplar strips are widely available in 1 × 2, 1 × 3, and 1 × 4 sizes.

Crown moldings (E, F) cover gaps between the top of a built-in and the ceiling. Crown molding also adds a decorative accent to a built-in.

Cove molding (G) is a simple, unobtrusive trim for covering gaps between a built-in project and a wall or ceiling.

Ornamental moldings, including spindle-and-rail (H) and embossed moldings (I, J), give a built-in a distinctive decorative look.

Door-edge molding (K), sometimes called cap molding, is used with finish-grade plywood to create panel-style doors and drawer faces.

Shelf-edge molding (L), sometimes called base cap molding, gives a decorative edge to plywood shelves.

Base shoe molding (M) covers gaps around the top, bottom, and sides of a built-in. Because it bends easily, base shoe molding works well to cover irregular gaps caused by uneven walls and floors.

Power tools used for constructing built-ins include: power miter saw (A), circular saw with general-purpose and hollow-ground blades (B), router with straight bits and decorative bits (C), power screw-driver (D), pad sander (E), jig saw with wood-cutting blades (F), belt sander (G), reciprocating saw (H), and drill with brad-point and forstner bits (I).

Tools & Fasteners

Most built-in projects can be constructed using ordinary hand and power tools you may already own. A large stationary tool, like a table saw, can be useful for a few tasks, but most projects in this book are designed so they can be built with simple tools and materials.

A well-constructed built-in project depends on accurate measuring, cutting, and fastening. Unless you have considerable experience, it is a good idea to practice your skills on scrap materials before starting a project.

A table saw is a good tool for making long rip cuts and bevel cuts. Table saws are available at some rental centers.

Hand tools you may need include: bar clamps (A), handsaw (B), level (C), framing square (D), wood mallet (E), handscrew clamps (F), putty knife (G), screwdrivers (H), hammer (I), chisel (J), paintbrush (K), marking gauge (L), tape measure (M), nail set (N), C-clamps (O), compass (P), utility knife (Q), plumb bob (R), stud finder (S), pencil (T), combination square (U), and hand sander (V).

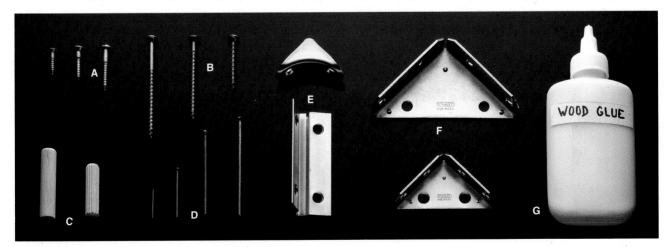

Fasteners you will need include: galvanized wood screws (A), power-driver wood screws designed for use with power screwdrivers (B), wood dowels (C), finish nails (D), metal corner brackets (E), countertop brackets (F), and wood glue (G).

Tool Accessories

A few tool accessories, some purchased and some made yourself, will help you work more accurately and quickly when constructing a built-in.

A straightedge guide like the one shown on the opposite page can be adapted to help you make perfectly straight cuts with a router, circular saw, or jig saw. The length of your straightedge guide depends on the size of the workpieces you will be cutting. Many do-it-yourselfers make straightedge guides in 2-ft., 4-ft., and 8-ft. lengths for convenience.

A portable clamping bench, like the Workmate®, can be moved easily to your work site to provide a convenient work surface. The Workmate has a jointed, adjustable table that tightens to clamp workpieces securely. Bench stops and horizontal clamps fit into openings in the bench surface, and adapt the Workmate to many uses.

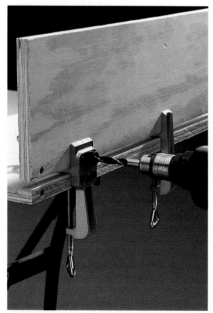

Dowel jig holds workpieces to ensure that drilled dowel holes will line up properly. (See page 34.)

Right-angle drill guide attached to a drill helps bore straight holes. The bit stop mounted on the guide lets you bore holes to an accurate and uniform depth.

Adjustable router edge guide attaches to the base of your router and helps make straight dado grooves within 6" of the edge of a workpiece.

1 Mark a straight, even line lengthwise onto a 10"-wide strip of 1/4" finish-grade plywood, about 4" from the edge. Cut a straight 1 × 2 cleat to the same length as the plywood strip.

2 Apply wood glue to the bottom of the cleat, then position it with one edge along the marked line on the plywood. Clamp one end of the cleat to the plywood, then add more clamps every 12", bending the cleat, if necessary, to follow the line. Let the glue dry, then remove the clamps.

Straightedge guide for a router: Create the proper setback by cutting off excess plywood with a router and straight bit, holding the base of the router firmly against the cleat. Make sure to cut with the same size bit you will be using in your projects; if you will be using more than one bit, make a separate straight-edge guide for each. (To use the straightedge guide, follow the technique shown on page 120.)

Straightedge guide for a circular saw: Create the proper setback by cutting off excess plywood with a circular saw. (To use the straightedge guide, follow the technique shown on page 120).

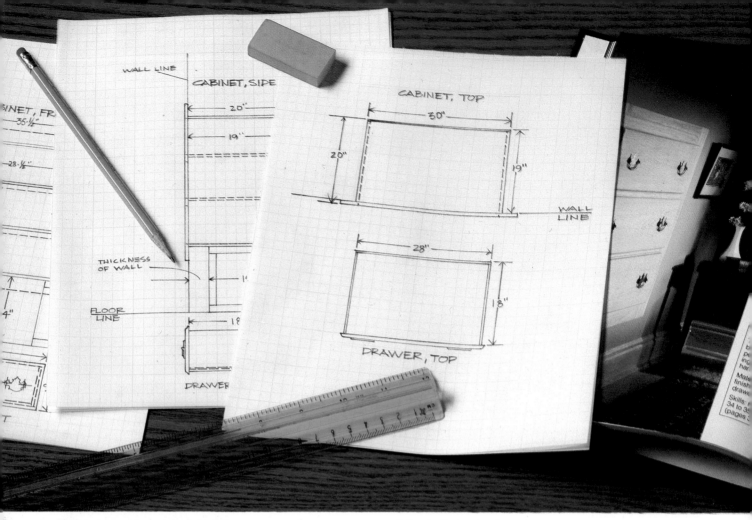

Make accurate scaled drawings on graph paper when adapting one of the built-in projects featured in this book. Use a simple scale, like 1 square = 1", to draw a side, top, and one or more front views of your project. For a complicated project, draw several front views showing the basic walls (carcass) of the built-in, the face frame construction, and the finished project including drawers and doors. Side views and top views should show all trim pieces and moldings. Make sure to use the actual measurements of sheet goods and dimension lumber when making your drawings.

Planning a Built-in Project

With each of the ten built-in projects found in this book, you can either build the project as shown, or adapt the design to fit your unique spaces and needs. To build the project as shown, follow the measurements in the parts table that accompanies each project. Small width and height adjustments can be made using the fitting tips on page 26.

In some cases, however, you may want to adapt a project design to create a larger or smaller built-in. If so, use the column of empty spaces next to the parts table to fill in your own measurements.

When adapting a built-in design, it is very important to make accurate plan drawings on graph paper to show how the project will fit in your space. These drawings let you organize your work and find approximate measurements for parts; they also make it easier to estimate the cost of materials.

To ensure a professional look and functional use, plan your built-ins so they fall within the standard range of sizes used by cabinet makers and furniture manufacturers (page opposite.)

Whether you are adapting a project or following a design as shown, it is safer to measure and cut the pieces as you assemble the built-in in its location, rather than to precut all pieces in advance. Small discrepancies in marking, cutting, and assembly techniques can lead to costly errors if you precut all the pieces.

Standard Built-in Measurements

Highest shelf should be no more than 80" above the floor to be within easy reach.

Shelves should be at least 10" deep in bookcases, and 12" deep in hanging wall cabinets. Space the shelves so there is at least 1¹/₂" of open space above the items you are storing.

First shelf in a wall-hung built-in should be at least 18" above a countertop.

Work-surface height varies depending on how the surface is used. Place the surface 24" above the floor for a typing desk or sewing work center. Place the countertop at 36" for standard kitchen cabinets, and at 44" for a dry bar or eating counter.

Standard seating surfaces, like window seats and desk chairs, are between 16" and 20" high.

Base cabinet depth varies from 15" for a room divider to 30" for cabinets that support a desk surface. Standard kitchen-style floor cabinets usually are 24" or 25" in depth.

Access space in front of a built-in should be at least 36" to provide kneeling space for opening drawers and cabinet doors.

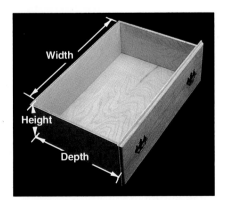

Drawer sizes range from a minimum of 3" high, 8" wide, and 8" deep; to a maximum of 10" high, 36" wide, and 30" deep. Large drawers, more than 24" wide, should be equipped with two drawer slides for stability.

Shown cutaway for clarity

Maximum height 80"

Minimum 18"

Sink

80

44"

36"

24"

36" minimum

15"

24"

30"

Fitting Tips for Built-ins

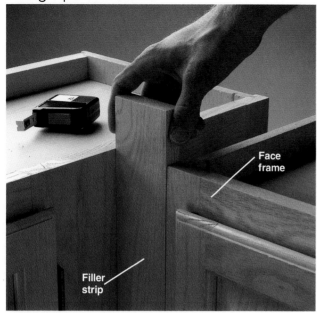

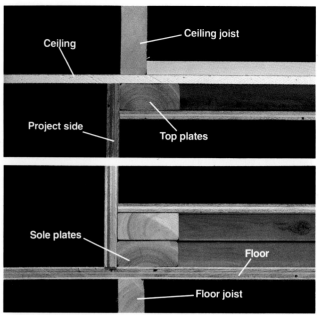

Make small width adjustments (up to 6" on each side) with hardwood strips measured and cut to fill the extra space. Attach the strips to the edges of the face frame with counterbored wood screws. These "filler strips" let you slightly enlarge a project without making changes to the basic design. Filler strips also can be scribed to fit uneven walls.

Make small height adjustments by changing the thickness of the sole plates or top plates that anchor the built-in to the floor and ceiling. The floor-to-ceiling projects in this book are designed to fit rooms with 8-ft. ceilings. If your room height differs slightly, adjusting the sole plates or top plates lets you adapt a project without major design changes.

Tips for Planning a Built-in Project

Nominal size	Actual size
1 × 2	3/4" × 1 1/2"
1 × 3	3/4" × 2 1/2"
1 × 4	3/4" × 3 1/2"
1 × 6	3/4" × 5 1/2"
1 × 8	3/4" × 7 1/4"
2 × 4	1 1/2" × 3 1/2"
2 × 6	1 1/2" × 5 1/2"
2 × 8	1 1/2" × 7 1/4"
2 × 10	1 1/2" × 9 1/4"

Measure spaces carefully. Floors, walls, and ceilings are not always level or plumb, so measure at several points. If measurements vary from point-to-point, use the shortest measurement to determine the height or width of your built-in.

Measure your materials. Actual thickness for plywood can vary from the listed nominal size; 3/4" plywood, for example, can vary in thickness by nearly 1/8".

Use actual measurements, not nominal measurements, of dimension lumber when planning a built-in. Table above shows the actual dimensions of common lumber.

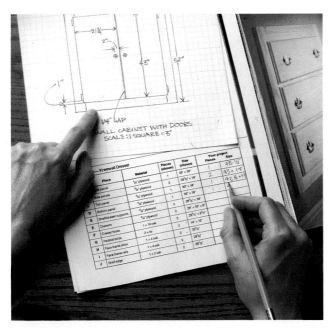

Revise the listed measurements of a featured project, if necessary, and write them down in the blank spaces found in the Parts List provided with each project. Use your scaled drawings as a guide for estimating the revised measurements. Always double-check measurements before cutting pieces to prevent costly cutting errors.

Make cutting diagrams to help you make efficient use of materials. Make scale drawings of sheet goods on graph paper, and sketch cutting lines for each part of your project. When laying out cutting lines, remember that the cutting path (kerf) of a saw blade can consume up to 1/8" of wood.

Materials	Amount needed	Cost for each	Total cost
Plywood (4 ft. × 8 ft.)			
1/4" sheets			
1/2" sheets			
3/4" sheets			
Lumber			
1 × 2 boards			
1 × 3 boards			
1 × 4 boards			
1 × 6 boards			
1 × 8 boards			
2 × 4s			
Moldings			
Door-edge			
Shelf-edge			
Base shoe			
Baseboard			
Crown/cove			
Ornamental			
Hardware			
Finish nails			
Power-driver screws			
Angle brackets			
Countertop brackets			
Drawer slides			
Hinges			
Door latches			
Pulls/knobs			
Other materials			
Wood glue			
Oil/stain			
Sanding sealer			
Paint			
Outlet strips			
Grommets			
Light fixtures			
Total cost:			$

Make a list of materials, using your plan drawings and cutting diagrams as a guide. Photocopy this materials list, and use it to organize your work and estimate costs.

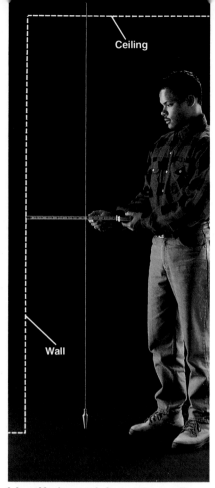

Use a cardboard template or a tape outline to mark the planned location of your built-in in the work area. If you discover that room corners are not square or that walls are uneven, you will need to purchase trim pieces, like base shoe or cove moldings, to cover gaps between the walls and your built-in project.

Identify bowed, irregular walls by hanging a plumb bob from the ceiling near the work area and measuring between the string and the wall at several points. Mark wall where distance is shortest; the built-in should be constructed so the back is plumb and flush at this point.

Preparing the Work Area

Before beginning a built-in project, take time to carefully evaluate and prepare your work area. Good preparation simplifies your work and ensures professional-looking results.

Locate and mark framing members in the project area so you can anchor your built-in securely. Where necessary, remove trim moldings and carpeting so the built-in will fit flush against walls. If a project will require you to cut into walls, pinpoint the location of electrical wires, plumbing pipes, and heating ducts before you begin.

Evaluate the walls and floor in the project area to see if they are square and straight. A common mistake made by many do-it-yourselfers is to alter a project design in an effort to make it fit irregular corners or walls that are badly out of plumb. Build your project so it is square, level, and plumb; then buy trim moldings to cover any gaps caused by leaning walls or sloping floors.

Locate studs and ceiling joists using an electronic stud finder. When passed over a plaster or wallboard surface, the stud finder pinpoints the edges of framing members by sensing changes in density.

Detach and roll back carpeting and pad before beginning construction, then trim to fit around the built-in after work is completed. Jute-back carpeting must be restretched and attached to new tackless strips. **NOTE:** If you have glued-down carpeting, it may be easier to install the built-in on top of the carpeting without removing it.

Remove baseboards and other moldings to make room for a built-in that will fit flush against a wall. Use a flat pry bar with a wood block to prevent damage to the wall, and pry carefully to avoid splintering the molding. After the built-in is installed, cut the molding to size, and reattach it.

Move electrical receptacles and other fixtures, if they are in the way of your planned built-in. You also may need to add receptacles for an entertainment center or other projects that require electrical service. **NOTE:** If you are not experienced at working with wiring, hire an electrician to do this work.

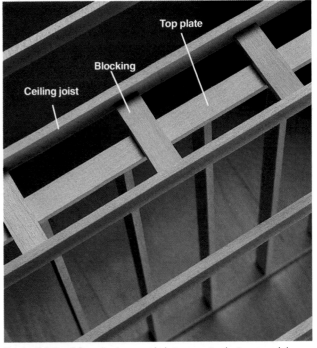

Install blocking between joists or studs to provide a solid surface for anchoring a built-in that does not line up with existing framing members. A room divider, for example, may require blocking between ceiling joists so it can be anchored to the ceiling.

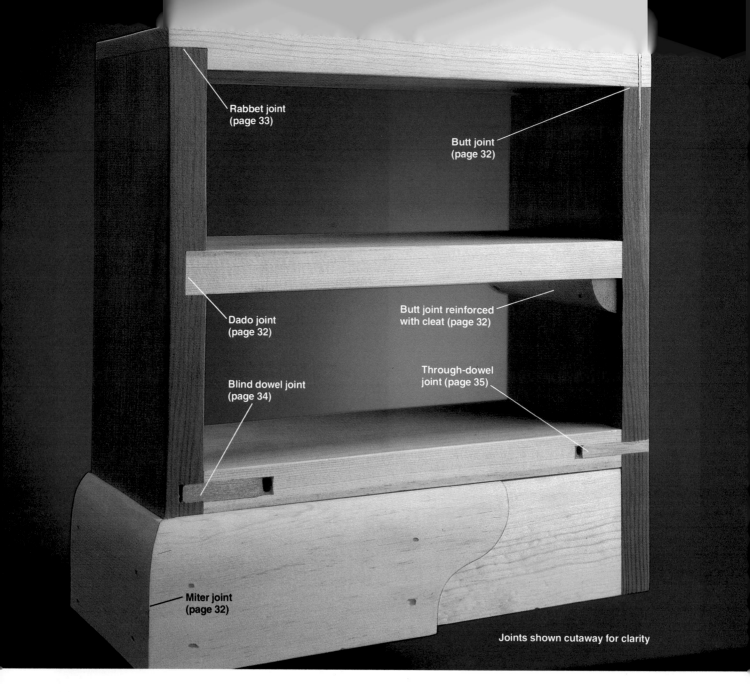

Rabbet joint
(page 33)

Butt joint
(page 32)

Dado joint
(page 32)

Butt joint reinforced
with cleat (page 32)

Through-dowel
joint (page 35)

Blind dowel joint
(page 34)

Miter joint
(page 32)

Joints shown cutaway for clarity

Making Joints

Joinery—the technique of creating strong, durable joints between separate pieces of wood—is essential to a successful built-in. Professional cabinet makers use dozens of joinery techniques, but a few simple joints shown on the following pages are all you need to construct the built-in projects featured in this book.

The joinery methods you choose depend on how the built-in will be used, and on the desired look. For example, a built-in used to display small items, like decorative glassware, can be made with simple butt joints reinforced with glue and finish nails. But a project that will hold heavy items, like a set of encyclopedias, should

be made with solid dado joints reinforced with screws. If appearance is very important, choose joinery techniques that conceal the methods of connection. For example, a built-in project constructed with blind dowel joints has a more professional look than one made with cleated butt joints.

For many built-ins, you will need to glue and clamp several joints at the same time—a job that requires a number and variety of clamps (page 21). For maximum strength and durability, use wood glue to reinforce all joints. Joints made with nails or screws alone are more likely to loosen over time.

Basic Gluing Techniques

Clean surfaces that will be glued, using a lint-free cloth. Smooth off any rough corners, using fine sandpaper.

Apply wood glue with a craft stick or dowel, spreading a thin, even layer over all surfaces that will be joined.

Slide glued surfaces back and forth against each other to create even contact and a firm bond.

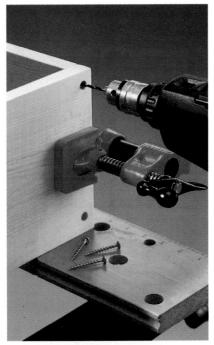

Clamp the pieces together to hold them securely while reinforcing joints. Check for squareness by measuring diagonals. If pieces are square, diagonals will have the same measurement. If diagonals differ, adjust the pieces until the diagonals are equal.

Reinforce joints by drilling pilot holes through the joint and driving screws or finish nails into the holes. For screws, counterbore the pilot holes so the screw heads can be driven below the surface. For nails, countersink the nail heads with a nail set (page 35).

Fill counterbored holes with glued hardwood plugs, and countersunk nail holes with wood putty. After glue or putty dries, sand the surface smooth, then apply finish (pages 46 to 49).

How to Make a Miter Joint

1 Mark moldings to the desired length, then set the blade on a miter saw to a 45° angle.

2 Hold or clamp the molding securely in the miter saw, then cut it to size. Apply a thin, even layer of wood glue to the mitered edges of the moldings.

3 Position the moldings on the workpiece with mitered ends tightly together. Drill pilot holes through the molding and into the workpiece, and attach the molding with finish nails.

How to Make Butt Joints

1 Outline the location of the joints on the workpiece, using a framing square as a guide. If desired, attach cleats (page 30) along the bottom edge of each joint to provide reinforcement.

2 Apply wood glue to the surfaces to be joined, using a craft stick or dowel to spread the glue evenly.

3 Position the pieces together, then reinforce each joint by drilling pilot holes and driving finish nails or screws through the joint. (Drawing a reference line on the workpiece can help you align the nails correctly.)

How to Make Dado Joints

1 Hold the pieces together and mark location of dado groove. Install a straight bit in a router, and set the bit to equal the depth of the planned dado. Dado depth generally is half as deep as the thickness of the wood; for 3/4"-thick wood, for example, dadoes should be 3/8" deep.

2 Clamp a straightedge guide (page 23) on each side of the planned dado, so the edges of the guides are against the marked lines. Set a piece of scrap wood the same thickness as the workpiece between the guides to check the spacing.

3 Cut the dado by making two passes with the router. Make the first pass with the base of the router held tightly against one straightedge cleat, then make the second pass in the opposite direction with the router base held against the other cleat.

How to Make Rabbet Joints

4 Apply wood glue to the surfaces being joined, then clamp the pieces together. Reinforce each joint by drilling pilot holes and driving screws or finish nails spaced 3" to 4" apart. For screws, counterbore the pilot holes with a larger drill bit.

Circular saw dadoes: Cut along the marked outline, using a straightedge guide (page 23) and circular saw with blade set to equal the depth of the dado. Then make several parallel cuts inside the edge cuts, and clean out waste wood with a sharp chisel.

Rabbet joints: Use a rabbet bit to rout edge grooves. Use a bit that is the same size as the thickness of the workpiece, and set the depth of cut to equal one-half the thickness. For example, for 3/4" workpieces, use a 3/4" rabbet bit set to 3/8" depth.

How to Make Blind Dowel Edge Joints Using a Dowel Jig

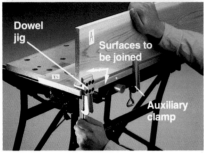

Surfaces to be joined

Dowel jig

Surfaces to be joined

Auxiliary clamp

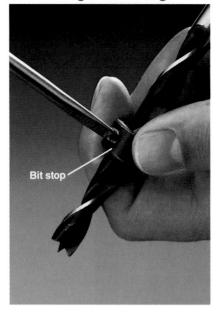

Bit stop

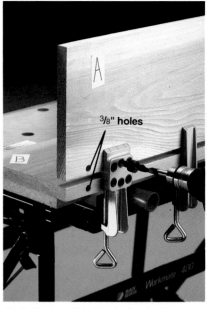

3/8" holes

1 Align pieces as they will look when the joint is finished, and mark them A and B (top). Reverse the position of the pieces as shown (bottom) so surfaces being joined are facing you. Clamp the pieces together so the ends are aligned, using a dowel jig and auxiliary clamp.

2 Mount a brad-point bit in a drill. Use a 3/8" bit if you will be doweling 3/4"-thick lumber. **TIP:** Attach a bit stop to the drill bit to ensure that you drill holes to the proper depth.

3 Drill dowel holes in both pieces through the jig opening that matches your bit size. For 3/4"-thick wood, holes in piece A should be 1/2" deep, and holes in B should be 1 1/4" deep. Reposition the jig and drill additional holes, spaced 3" to 4" apart. Leave auxiliary clamp in place when moving jig.

4 Test-fit the pieces by inserting fluted 1 1/2" dowels in piece A, then tapping piece B in place with a wood mallet. If pieces do not fit tightly, deepen the dowel holes in piece B.

5 Separate pieces and remove dowels, then apply glue to the dowels and insert them into holes in piece B. Also apply glue to the flat surfaces being joined. **NOTE:** When joining melamine-covered particleboard, apply glue to dowels only, not to the flat surfaces.

6 Assemble the pieces, tapping them with a wood mallet until the joint is snug. Completely wipe away any excess glue, using a damp cloth.

How to Make Blind Dowel Face Joints Using Dowel Centers

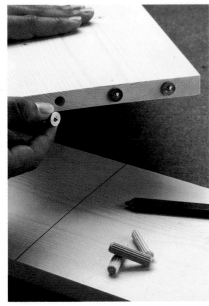  

1 Mark the face of the workpiece to show location of joint. Make edge holes for dowels with a dowel jig (page opposite), then insert a dowel center in each hole.

2 Stand the pieces on edge on a flat surface, then force the pieces together so the sharp points on the dowel centers leave reference marks in the wood.

3 Drill holes at marked points, using a brad-point bit. For 3/4"-thick wood, holes should be 1/2" deep. Use a right-angle drill guide with bit stop to ensure straight, uniform holes. Assemble the workpiece with dowels (steps 4 to 6, page opposite).

How to Make Through-dowel Joints

1 Clamp and glue pieces together, and make a reference line to help you align the dowel holes. Then use a brad-point bit with a bit stop set to 13/4" depth to drill dowel holes through one piece and into the adjoining piece. Space the holes 3" to 4" apart.

2 Apply wood glue to fluted 11/2" dowels, then insert the dowels into the holes. Drive the dowels to the bottoms of the holes, using a nail set.

3 Fill dowel holes with hardwood plugs coated with wood glue (page 31). Let the glue dry, then sand the plugged surface smooth.

¼" glass

Melamine-covered
particleboard

¾" pine

¾" finish-grade
plywood

¾" hardwood

¾" finish-grade
plywood edged
with 1 × 2
hardwood

Double-layer
plywood edged
with hardwood
molding

**Shelves shown in
order of strength**

Adding Shelves

When making shelves for your built-in projects, choose shelving materials appropriate for the loads they must support. Thin glass shelves or particleboard can easily support light loads, like decorative glassware, but only the sturdiest shelves can hold a large television set or heavy reference books without bending or breaking.

The strength of a shelf also depends on its span—the distance between vertical risers. In general, shelves should be no more than 36" long.

Some shelves in built-ins are permanent features, joined to the body of the built-in using basic joinery methods (pages 30 to 35). Other shelves are adjustable, mounted with metal brackets or pin-style shelf supports. Adjustable shelves give more versatile storage, but permanent shelves are stronger. Permanent shelves also add structural reinforcement that improves the overall sturdiness of a built-in. Many built-ins include both permanent shelves for structural strength, and adjustable shelves for versatility.

Building your own shelves from finish-grade plywood edged with hardwood strips or moldings is a good choice for most built-in projects. Edged plywood shelves are strong, attractive, and much less expensive than solid hardwood shelves.

Attach hardwood edging or moldings to the front face of plywood shelves, using wood glue and finish nails. Position the edging so the top is slightly above the plywood surface, then drill pilot holes and drive finish nails. Use a nail set to countersink the nail heads. Sand the edging so it is smooth with the plywood surface before you finish the shelf (page 48). For greater strength, edge plywood shelves with 1 × 2 or 1 × 3 hardwood boards (photo, left).

How to Install Pin-style Supports for Adjustable Shelves

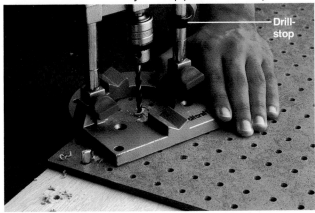

1 Mount a drill and 1/4" bit in a right-angle drill guide, with drill-stop set for 3/8" depth. Align a pegboard scrap along the inside face of each riser, exactly flush with the end, to use as a template. Drill two rows of parallel holes in each riser, about 1 1/2" from the edges of riser, using the pegboard holes as a guide.

2 When built-in is completed, build shelves that are 1/8" shorter than the distance between risers. To mount each shelf, insert a pair of 1/4" pin-style shelf supports in each riser.

How to Install Metal Standards for Adjustable Shelves

1 Mark two parallel dado grooves on the inside face of each riser, using a marking gauge. Grooves should be at least 1" from the edges.

2 Cut dadoes to depth and thickness of metal standards, using a router (page 23). Test-fit standards to make sure they fit, then remove them.

3 After finishing the built-in, cut metal standards to fit into dadoes, and attach using nails or screws provided by manufacturer. Make sure slots in standards are aligned properly so shelves will be level.

4 Build shelves 1/8" shorter than the distance between risers, then insert shelf clips into the slots on the metal standards, and install shelves.

Adding Doors

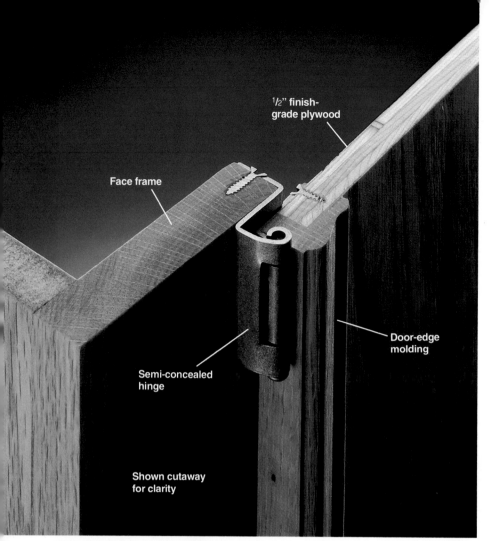

½" finish-grade plywood

Face frame

Semi-concealed hinge

Door-edge molding

Shown cutaway for clarity

Easy-to-build overlay doors, made with ½" finish-grade plywood panels framed with door-edge moldings, are designed to overhang the face frame by about ³⁄₈" on each side. Semi-concealed overlay hinges, which require no mortising, are attached to the back of the door and to the edge of the face frame. This door style also can be adapted to make folding doors (page 117).

Cabinet doors are easy to make using ½" finish-grade plywood, and door-edge moldings. When hung with semi-concealed overlay hinges, do-it-yourself panel-style doors require no complicated routing or mortising techniques. You can build them to any size needed, and finish them to match your tastes.

Another easy option is to buy ready-made cabinet doors from a cabinet manufacturer or cabinet refacing company, and hang them yourself using semi-concealed hinges. You also can have a professional cabinetmaker design and build custom cabinet doors to your specifications—a good choice if you want wood-framed doors with glass panels.

Other do-it-yourself door options include sliding doors, solid-glass doors, and frameless doors (page opposite).

Door-catch hardware is recommended if your doors do not use self-closing hinges, or if you want to lock them. Common types of hardware include: utility hasp (A), roller catch (B), keyed lock (C), brass door bolt (D), and magnetic push latch (E) commonly used for solid glass doors.

Door Options

Ready-made cabinet doors are available in stock sizes from cabinet manufacturers and cabinet refacing companies. Or, you can have doors custom-built by a professional cabinetmaker. Install these doors with semi-concealed overlay hinges (steps 5 to 9, pages 40 to 41).

Sliding doors are a good choice if limited space makes it impractical to install swinging doors. Build a pair of sliding doors from 1/4" finish-grade plywood, cut so they are 1/2" shorter than the opening and will overlap by about 2" in the center. Attach door-track moldings to the top, bottom, and sides of the door opening. Install the doors by sliding them up into the top track, then lowering them into the bottom track.

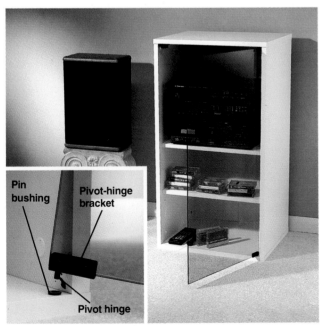

Pin
bushing

Pivot-hinge
bracket

Pivot hinge

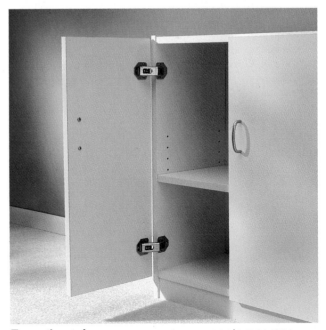

Glass doors give a contemporary look to built-in projects. Use 1/4" tempered glass with smoothed edges, not ordinary window glass, for doors. To install a glass door, drill holes in the top and bottom of the door opening, and insert pivot-hinge bushings. Mount the door using pivot-hinge brackets attached to the glass with setscrews (inset).

Frameless doors are common on contemporary-style built-ins constructed without face frames—especially those made with melamine-covered particleboard. Frameless doors are mounted with concealed hinges attached to the inside surface of the built-in.

1 Measure the width and height of the door opening, and cut one or two door panels from 1/2" finish-grade plywood. (If opening is wider than 24", two doors are necessary.) **For two doors:** each door panel should equal the measured height of the opening; width of each panel will be one-half the total width of the opening, minus 1/2". (For example, if opening is 14" high and 36" wide, each door panel should be 14" high and 17 1/2" wide.) **For one door:** door panel should equal the width and height of the door opening.

2 For each door, measure and cut door-edge molding to frame the door panel, mitering the ends at a 45° angle.

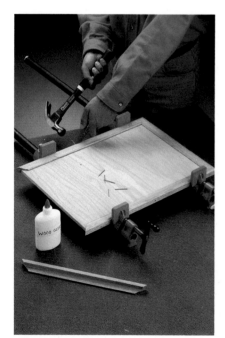

3 Attach door-edge molding to door panel by drilling pilot holes and driving 1 1/2" finish nails through the side of the molding and into the door panels. Finish the door to match the built-in.

4 Mount two semi-concealed overlay hinges to the back of the door, 2" from the top and bottom. **NOTE:** Use three hinges, evenly spaced, if the door is taller than 30".

5 Use masking tape to mark a reference line on the top face frame rail, 1/2" above the door opening.

6 Position the door over the opening, aligning the top edge with the tape reference line. Mark one hinge location on the face frame with masking tape.

7 Open the hinges, and position the door against the edge of the face frame so the hinge is aligned with the tape marking the hinge locations. Drill pilot holes, and anchor the hinges to the face frame with the mounting screws. Remove the masking tape.

8 Attach door handles or knobs, and any door catch hardware you desire, following manufacturer's directions.

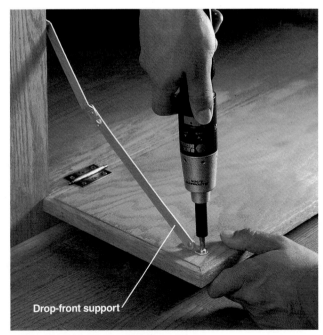

Drop-front support

Drop-down door variation: Build an overlay door as directed above, but attach the semi-concealed hinges to the bottom face frame rail. Attach drop-front supports on both sides of the door opening to support the door, and install door-catch hardware to keep it from falling open.

Adding Drawers

Most built-ins can be adapted to include drawers. In addition to providing useful storage, drawers and decorative hardware make a built-in more attractive.

In its simplest form, a drawer is nothing more than a wooden box that slides back and forth on a permanent shelf. By adding drawer slide hardware, a hardwood drawer face, and ornamental knobs or pulls, you can make drawers look more professional.

Ready-made hardwood drawer faces are sold by companies specializing in cabinet refacing products. Or, you can make your own drawer faces by cutting hardwood boards and using a router to give them decorative edges.

Drawers can be constructed in many different styles, but the drawer shown on the following pages is simple to build and will work for any of the built-in projects in this book. This design is called an "overlay" drawer because it features a hardwood drawer face that overhangs the cabinet face frame by 1/2".

Drawer pulls and knobs help define the overall style of your project. If your built-in also includes cabinet doors with handles or pulls, buy all door and drawer hardware at the same time to ensure a good match. For drawers wider than 24", install two knobs or pulls.

Tips for Building Drawers

Drawer bottom and cabinet face frame shown cutaway for clarity

Choose center-mounted drawer slides with steel ball-bearing rollers. Center-mounted slides, like the Accuride® slide shown above, are easier to install than side-mounted slides, and those with steel ball-bearings are much more durable than those with plastic rollers. Specify the depth of your drawers when buying drawer slides.

Make your own drawer faces by cutting hardwood boards to the proper size, then routing ornamental edges on them with a decorative router bit, like an ogee bit. To ensure smooth edges, make the cuts with several passes of the router; begin with the bit set to a shallow depth, then gradually extend the bit until you achieve the desired appearance.

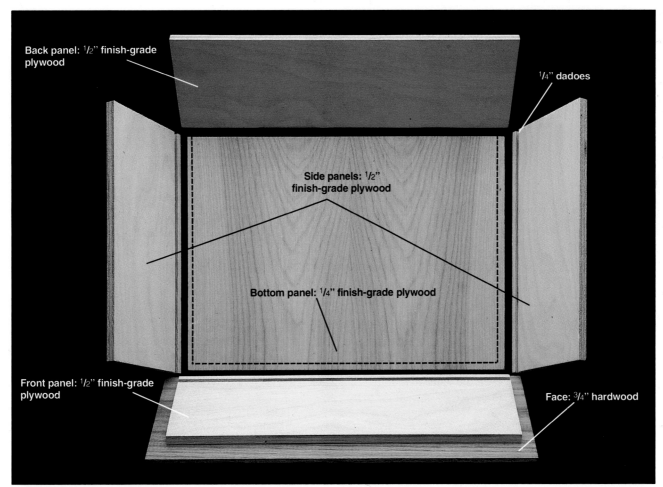

Back panel: 1/2" finish-grade plywood

Side panels: 1/2" finish-grade plywood

1/4" dadoes

Bottom panel: 1/4" finish-grade plywood

Front panel: 1/2" finish-grade plywood

Face: 3/4" hardwood

Anatomy of an overlay drawer: The basic drawer box is made using 1/2" plywood for the front, back, and side panels, with a 1/4" plywood bottom panel. The bottom panel fits into 1/4" dadoes cut near the bottom of the front and side panels, and is nailed to the bottom edge of the back panel. The hardwood drawer face is screwed to the drawer front from the inside, and is sized so it overhangs the face frame by 1/2" on all sides. **NOTE:** This drawer is designed to be mounted with a center-mounted drawer slide attached to the bottom of the drawer (page opposite). If you use different hardware, like side-mounted drawer slides, you will need to alter this design according to slide manufacturer's directions.

How to Measure for an Overlay Drawer

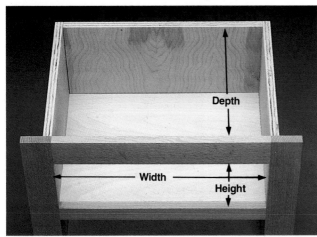

Depth

Width

Height

Part		Measurement
Sides	length	Depth of opening, minus 3"
	height	Height of opening, minus 1/2"
Front	length	Width of opening, minus 1 1/2"
	height	Height of opening, minus 1/2"
Back	length	Width of opening, minus 1 1/2"
	height	Height of opening, minus 1"
Bottom	width	Width of opening, minus 1"
	depth	Depth of opening, minus 2 3/4"
Face	length	Width of opening, plus 1"
	height	Height of opening, plus 1"

1 Measure the width and height of the face frame opening, and the depth of the cabinet from face frame to back panel.

2 Calculate the sizes for each drawer part using the table above. Cut and assemble the drawer by following the directions on the following pages.

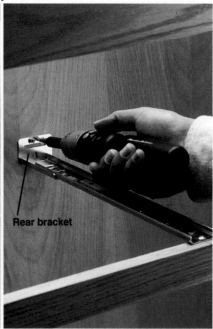

Rear bracket

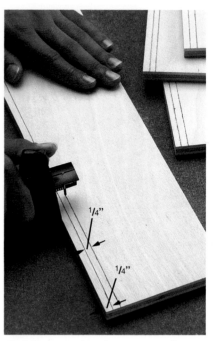

¼"

¼"

1 Install the track for the center-mounted drawer slide, as directed by the manufacturer. If the slide track will rest on a permanent shelf (left), it is easiest to install it on the shelf before assembling the built-in. If the slide will be supported by the face frame and the back panel (right), mount the slide using the rear bracket included with the drawer slide kit.

2 Measure the drawer opening, then cut all drawer pieces to size (page 43). Outline ¼"-wide dado grooves on the inside faces of the side and front panels, ¼" from the bottom edges, using a marking gauge as a guide.

Router edge guide

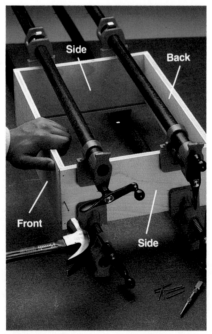

Side

Back

Front

Side

3 Cut ¼" deep dadoes along the marked outlines, using a router and ¼" straight bit. Use a router edge guide (page 23) to ensure straight cuts.

4 Clamp and glue the front, back, and side panels together, so front and back panels are between the side panels, and the top edges of panels are aligned. Reinforce each corner with 2" finish nails driven through the joints.

5 Let glue dry, then remove the clamps. From the back of the drawer box, slide the drawer bottom panel fully into the dado grooves. Do not apply glue to the dadoes or the bottom panel.

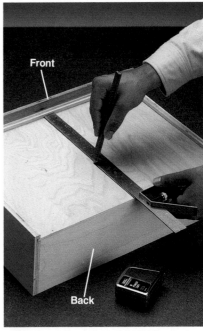

6 Attach the rear edge of the bottom panel to the back panel with wire nails spaced every 4".

7 Position the drawer box against the back side of the drawer face, so the face overhangs by 1/2" on the sides and bottom, and 1" on the top. Attach the face with 1" screws driven into the drawer face from inside the drawer box.

8 Lay the drawer upside down, then measure and mark a center line along the bottom panel from front to back.

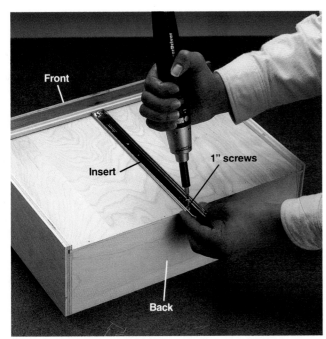

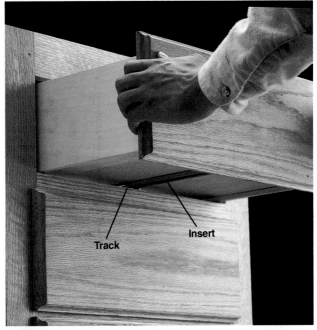

9 Center the drawer slide insert over the marked center line, and attach it with a 1" screw driven through the drawer bottom and into the back panel, and another screw driven diagonally into the drawer front panel.

10 Install the drawer by lining up the insert with the track, then gently pushing the drawer in until the insert and track lock together. Attach drawer pulls or knobs, if desired.

Finishing a Built-in

Careful finishing work on a built-in is as important as the construction. Good finishing improves the appearance of the built-in, protects the wood, and hides small errors and imperfections.

All finishing work for a built-in consists of three equally important stages: filling gaps and nail holes; sanding and cleaning; and applying a top-coat finish of tinted oil or stain. All wood products, even finish-grade plywood and presanded hardwood boards, need to be sanded and cleaned before they are top-coated.

Generally, it is easiest to apply finish or paint after the built-in project is assembled, but for complicated projects, especially those with deep shelves, consider sanding and finishing the pieces individually before assembling them.

A traditional wood finish is made from successive coats of sealer, stain, and several coats of varnish or shellac; but a variety of newer one-step finishes produce excellent results, and are much quicker and easier to apply. Most one-step finishes have an oil base, but a growing number are latex products with a water base. For heavy-use surfaces, like a dining counter, you can cover a one-coat finish with a layer of clear polyurethane.

One-step wood finishes include (from left to right): rubbing oil/finish—a combination of tinted penetrating oil and semigloss tung oil; pure tung oil finish—a clear, semigloss finish often used to protect bare wood; and Danish oil—a penetrating, nongloss oil available in many tints. When choosing a tinted one-step finish, choose a color that matches other woodwork in your home, and always test the finish on scrap wood before you begin.

Specialty tools and materials for finishing work include: 120-grit sanding belt (A), staining pad (B), untinted wood filler (C), clear polyurethane (D), tack cloth (E), finish-nail holder (F), tinted filler sticks (G, H), paintbrush with blended bristles (I), putty knife (J), and sandpaper in 80-, 120-, and 220-grit sheets (K).

Painted finishes require a primer coat of sanding sealer to provide a smooth undercoat, followed by one or two coats of latex enamel or oil-base enamel. Latex enamel is easy to apply and clean up, but better grades of oil-base enamel create a smoother finished surface.

Finishing Tips

Protect walls from stains by sliding a sheet of wax paper or plastic between the trim moldings and the wall before applying oil finish or paint.

Scrape away dried glue before painting or finishing, using an old chisel with the corners rounded off. Finishing oils and paint will not penetrate glue, so any excess must be removed completely before finish is applied.

Use a toothbrush to apply finishes to hard-to-reach areas, like spindle-and-rail moldings and other ornamental trim pieces.

Protect surfaces that will be glued, if you are finishing the pieces before assembling the built-in. Glue will not bond to oiled or stained wood, so cover joint areas with masking tape before applying finishing materials.

Use a tinted filler stick to fill nail holes in finished wood. Filler sticks come in many tones, but if none matches the finish of your built-in exactly, blend putty from different sticks to create the color you need.

Use heat-activated veneer tape to cover unfinished edges of plywood or particleboard panels on built-ins without face frames. Bond the tape with a household iron, then rub the tape with a block of hardwood. Trim the overhang with a utility knife, then lightly sand the edges to smooth them.

Preparation Tips

Fill nail holes and gaps in wood surfaces, using untinted wood filler. Let the filler dry completely before sanding the surfaces. On plywood surfaces that will be painted, fill any void areas along exposed edges.

Sand hardwood face frames to smooth the joints and remove surface defects. First, sand with a belt sander and 80-grit sanding belt (left), using light pressure to avoid gouging the wood. Then sand with a pad sander and 120-grit sandpaper (right). Change to 220-grit sandpaper for the final sanding. Always move the sander in the same direction as the wood grain, and replace sanding sheets as they become worn.

Sand edged plywood shelves carefully. To avoid sanding through the surface veneer, make light pencil marks on the plywood surface next to the hardwood edging, then sand across the top of the edging just until the pencil marks are removed.

Use a hand sanding block and 220-grit sandpaper to sand corners and other areas where the pad sander will not fit.

Clean all sanded surfaces with a brush and vacuum, then wipe them with a tack cloth.

How to Apply One-step Finishes

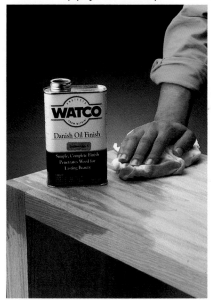  

Danish oil: Shake container thoroughly, then apply a heavy coat of oil to all wood surfaces, using a lint-free cloth. Wait 30 minutes, then apply more oil. Wait 15 minutes, then wipe the wood dry with clean rags.

Tung oil: Wipe a thin layer of tung oil onto the wood surface with a clean, folded cloth, rubbing in the direction of the wood grain. Wait 5 minutes, then buff the surface with a clean, lint-free cloth. Let the finish harden for 24 hours, then apply a second coat of tung oil.

Rubbing oil/finish: Shake container thoroughly, then apply a heavy coat to all surfaces, using a staining pad. Wait 5 minutes, then wipe away excess with a clean rag. Let finish harden for 2 hours, then apply a second coat. Apply extra coats, 2 hours apart, if you wish to darken the finish.

How to Apply Enamel Paint

1 After sanding and cleaning wood surfaces, apply a thick coat of sanding sealer to all surfaces that will be painted. Let the sealer dry for 3 hours.

2 Sand surfaces with 220-grit sandpaper, and wipe away all dust with a tack cloth. Apply additional coats of sealer, sanding after each coat, until wood grain feels perfectly smooth to the touch. Open-grain woods, like pine, require several coats of sealer.

3 Wipe surfaces clean of all sanding dust, then apply enamel paint, brushing in the same direction as the wood grain. Let the paint dry for 2 hours, then sand lightly with 220-grit sandpaper and apply a second coat of paint.

Halogen lights

Wire
tracks

Add low-voltage light fixtures to highlight favorite items and add visual interest to any built-in project. Low-voltage halogen lights, like those shown above, use very little electricity, and can be left on permanently. Wires for low-voltage lights run through small dado grooves cut into the shelves and risers, and are covered with plastic wire tracks inserted in the dadoes. Leave several inches of open space between lights and stored items to prevent heat from building up.

Adding Electrical Accessories

Transformer

Adding electrical accessories to your built-in projects makes them more attractive and useful. An ordinary bookcase becomes an elegant display case when you add built-in lighting fixtures. Installing a convenient electrical outlet strip in the back of an entertainment center lets you connect electronic equipment without using cumbersome, dangerous extension cords.

When adding lights or other electrical accessories to a built-in, try to position the wires so they are hidden from view. Inexpensive plastic wire organizers and wire tracks attached inside a built-in help hide electrical cords and prevent them from tangling.

A 12-volt transformer converts 120-volt current from an ordinary wall receptacle to provide power for low-voltage lights, like those shown above.

Helpful Electrical Accessories

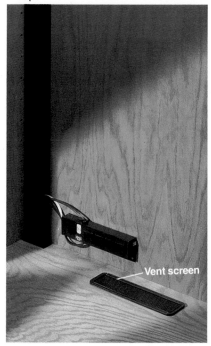

Install vent screens in the shelves or walls of your built-in to help dissipate heat if your built-in will contain electronic equipment, like a television, computer, stereo, or microwave oven.

An outlet strip attached inside a built-in provides a convenient place to plug in a television, stereo, computer, or light fixtures. Some models have a remote on-off switch to control up to four receptacles, and may include a telephone jack or cable TV outlet. Outlet strips with power-surge protection are essential for use with a computer.

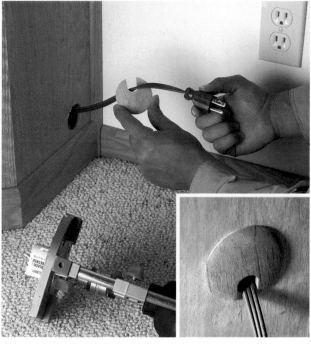

A wire organizer tacked inside a built-in hides and organizes electrical cords and cables. Wire organizers are made of plastic, and can be cut to any length you need.

Grommet plates help hide the holes that have been drilled to run cords and cables through the sides of a built-in. Drill the holes with a hole saw or forstner bit to reduce splintering. Grommets are available in a variety of materials, including hardwood, which can be finished to match most wood surfaces (inset).

Built-In Projects

See page 9 for more ideas for using recessed wall shelves

Building Recessed Wall Shelves

Installing recessed shelving is one of the easiest built-in projects. This project consists of a shallow wooden box that is inserted in a wall cutout and framed with hardwood. Recessed shelves can be installed in almost any interior wall, except in areas where electrical wires or plumbing pipes are located.

The project as shown is 30" wide—the width of two stud cavities in a standard wall built with studs spaced 16" on-center. To duplicate these shelves, you will need to cut away one wall stud

and install a sill and header. Never cut away more than one stud when building recessed shelving. You may, however, build a narrower cabinet by building the shelves into a single stud cavity between adjacent studs.

Everything You Need:

Tools: pencil, level, jig saw, reciprocating saw, power screwdriver, drill, right-angle drill guide, pegboard scraps, pipe clamps, hammer, tape measure, utility knife.

Materials: wood glue, finish nails (1½", 3"), wood screws (1½", 2½"), 1" wire nails, pin-style shelf supports, wood shims.

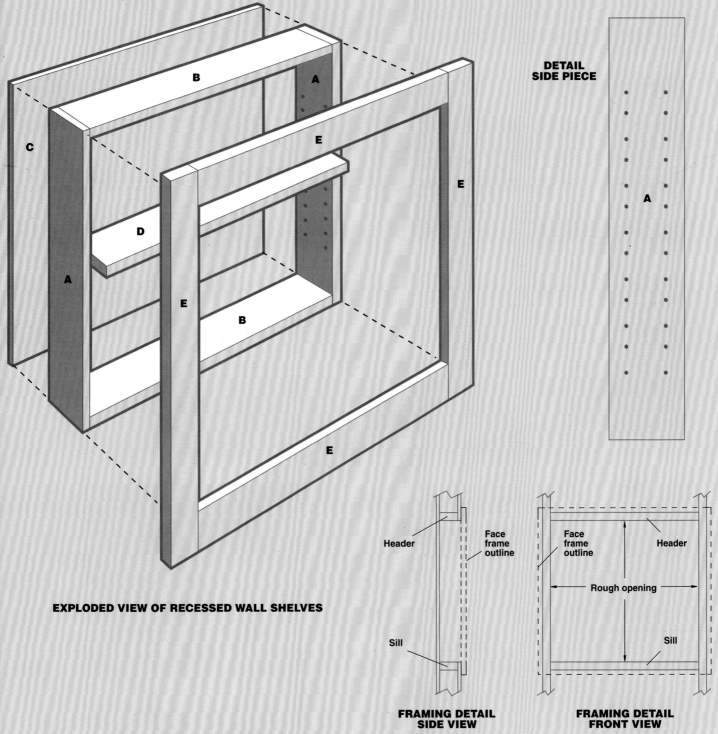

DETAIL SIDE PIECE

A

B

A

C

E

D

A

E

B

E

E

EXPLODED VIEW OF RECESSED WALL SHELVES

Header

Face frame outline

Sill

FRAMING DETAIL SIDE VIEW

Face frame outline

Header

Rough opening

Sill

FRAMING DETAIL FRONT VIEW

Parts List: Recessed Wall Shelves

Project as Shown					Your Project	
Key	**Piece**	**Material**	**Pieces**	**Size**	**Pieces**	**Size**
A	Sides	1 × 4 oak	2	30"		
B	Top & bottom	1 × 4 oak	2	28¾"		
C	Back panel	¼" oak plywood	1	30 × 30¼"		
D	Shelves	1 × 4 oak	3	28⅝"		
E	Face frame	1 × 4 oak	11 linear ft.			
F	Header and sill plates	2 × 4	2	30½"		

How to Build Recessed Shelving

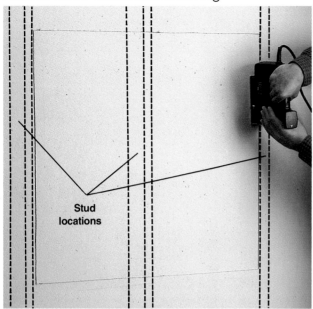

1 Locate wall studs in area where shelves will be installed. Mark the cutout on the wall, using a level as a guide. Sides of cutout should follow edges of wall studs, and height of cutout should allow for the thickness of a header and sill plate. Make the cutout with a jigsaw. **CAUTION:** Check for plumbing and electrical cables before cutting into any wall.

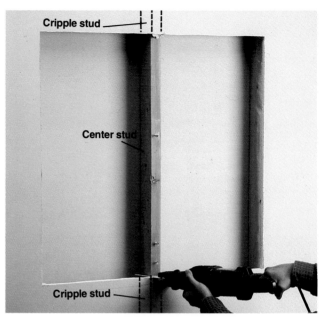

2 Cut away the center stud at the top and bottom edge of the opening, using a reciprocating saw. Use a flat pry bar to remove the cut portion of stud. (You may need to patch the opposite wall surface if it is screwed or nailed to the stud you remove.)

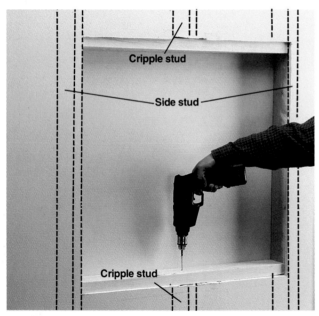

3 Measure between side studs at top and bottom edges of opening, and cut header and sill plates to fit. Attach header and sill to cripple studs and side studs with 3" screws. Remeasure the height of the opening between the installed header and sill plates. Cut side pieces ¼" shorter than measured height of the opening. Cut top and bottom pieces 1¾" shorter than the measured width to allow for small adjustments during installation.

4 Drill two rows of holes on the inside face of each side piece to hold pin-style shelf supports (page 37). Use a right-angle drill guide, and use a scrap piece of pegboard as a template to ensure that the holes on facing pieces will be lined up properly.

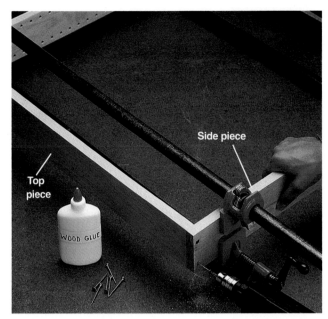

5 Glue and clamp the side pieces around the top and bottom pieces to form butt joints (page 32). Drill counterbored pilot holes into the joints, and reinforce them with 1½" wood screws.

6 Measure and cut ¼" plywood back panel to fit flush with the outside edges of the frame. Position the panel with the grain running vertically. Attach with 1" wire nails driven every 4 or 5". To allow for natural expansion and contraction, do not glue the back panel.

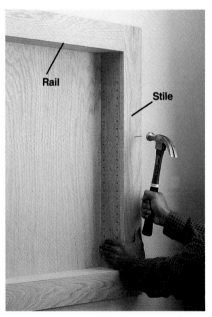

7 Position box in opening and shim until it is level and plumb and front edges are flush with wall surface. Drill pilot holes, and anchor cabinet to side studs, header and sill, using 1½" finish nails driven every 4" to 5" and through shim locations. Trim shims with a utility knife.

8 Measure the inside height and width of cabinet box, then cut 1 × 4 horizontal face frame rails equal to width, and 1 × 4 vertical stiles 7" longer than height. Glue and clamp rails between stiles to form butt joints, and reinforce joints by drilling angled pilot holes and toenailing 3" finish nails through stiles and into rails.

9 Position face frame, drill pilot holes, and attach with 1½" finish nails driven into the top, bottom, and side panels, and into the framing members. Countersink nails, fill nail holes, sand, and finish the project (pages 46 to 49). Build and install adjustable shelves (page 37) ⅛" shorter than distance between side panels.

Building a Kneewall Cabinet

A kneewall is a short wall that meets the slope of the roofline in an upstairs room. By cutting a hole in a kneewall and installing a recessed cabinet, you can turn the wasted space behind it into a useful storage area.

Because the body (carcass) of a kneewall cabinet is not visible, it can be built using ordinary plywood and simple butt joints. The face frame and drawer faces, however, should be built with hardwood, and finished carefully.

The project shown here fits in a space that is 30" wide—the standard width of two adjacent stud cavities with a center stud removed. Before beginning work, check the spacing of studs and the location of electrical or plumbing lines behind your kneewall. Your kneewall may have a removable access panel, which makes it easy to check behind the wall.

You can make the cabinet wider or narrower to fit your wall stud spacing, but regardless of size, be sure to leave a few inches of space between the back of the cabinet and the rafters.

Everything You Need:

Tools: level, circular saw or jigsaw, flat pry bar, reciprocating saw, drill, tape measure, bar clamps, hammer, nail set.

Materials: power-driver screws (1", 2", 3"), finish nails (1 1/2", 2", 3"), wood glue, finishing materials, drawer hardware.

See page 8 for more kneewall cabinet ideas

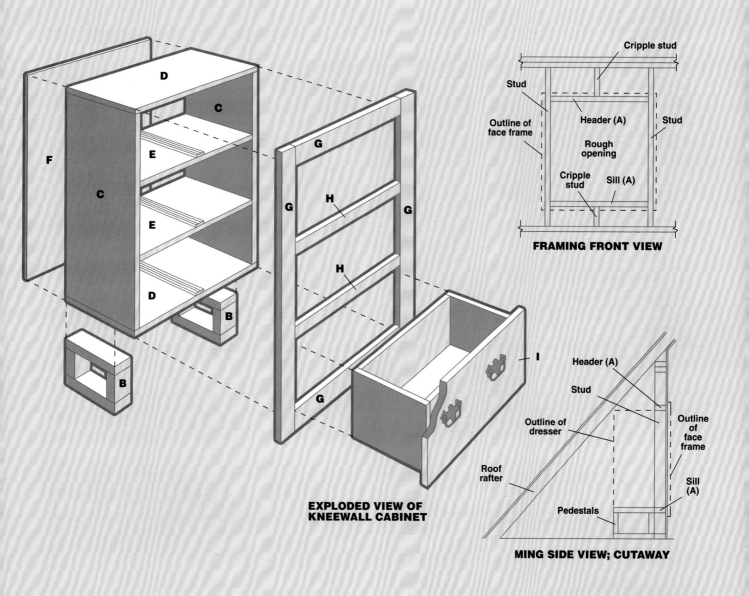

FRAMING FRONT VIEW

EXPLODED VIEW OF KNEEWALL CABINET

MING SIDE VIEW; CUTAWAY

Parts List: Kneewall Cabinet

		Project as Shown				Your Project	
Key	**Part**	**Material**	**Pieces**	**Size**		**Pieces**	**Size**
A	Header and sill	2 × 4s	6 linear ft.				
B	Pedestals	2 × 4s	2	14" × 15"			
C	Sides	3/4" plywood	2	28 1/2" × 19"			
D	Top and bottom	3/4" plywood	2	30" × 19"			
E	Shelves	3/4" plywood	2	28 1/2" × 19"			
F	Back panel	1/4" plywood	1	30" × 30"			
G	Face frame	1 × 4 oak	11 linear ft.				
H	Shelf rails	1 × 2 oak	5 linear ft.				
I	Drawers	see pages 42 to 55					

Kneewall Cabinet Project Details

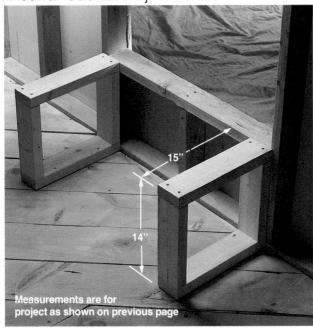

15"

14"

Pedestals installed behind the kneewall create a sturdy base for the cabinet. Built from 2 × 4s, the pedestals raise the cabinet so it fits above the baseboard. Raising the cabinet also makes drawers more accessible.

1 × 2 shelf rails

1 × 4 rails

8½" × 28½" opening

1 × 4 stiles

Face frame is 1 × 4 hardwood, which will cover the rough edges of the wall opening. The shelf rails are made from 1 × 2 hardwood to maximize the size of the drawer openings.

How to Build a Kneewall Cabinet

1 Locate wall studs in area where cabinet will be installed. Mark the cutout on the wall, using a level as a guide. Bottom of cutout should be at least 3" above baseboard, and sides of cutout should follow edges of wall studs. Height of cutout should be 3¼" taller than overall height of cabinet, to allow space for a header and sill. **CAUTION:** Check for wiring, pipes, and duct work before cutting into any wall.

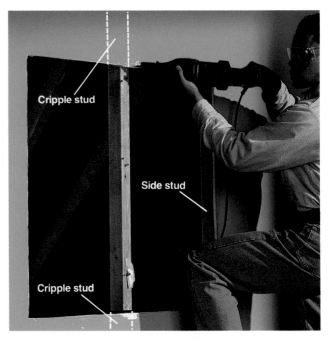

Cripple stud

Side stud

Cripple stud

2 Cut away the center stud at the top and bottom of the opening, using a reciprocating saw. Remove the stud. Remaining portions of cut studs are called "cripple" studs.

60

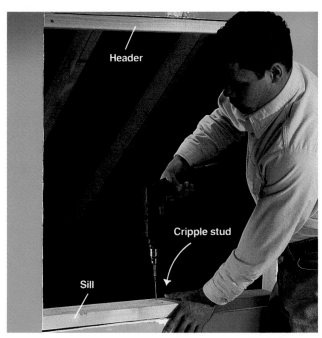

3 Measure and cut a 2 × 4 header and sill to fit snugly between side studs. Position in opening, check for level, and shim if necessary. Attach the header and sill to the cripple studs and side studs, using 3" screws.

4 Measure the distance from the floor behind the opening to the top of the sill, and build two 2 × 4 pedestals to this height (see Project Details, page 60). Join pedestal pieces together with glue and 3" screws.

5 Set the pedestals on the floor inside the wall opening, even with the sides of the framed opening. Check to make sure pedestals are level, and shim between the pedestals and the floor if necessary. Attach pedestals to the floor, using 3" screws.

6 Measure width and height of the rough opening between framing members. Cut side panels 2" shorter than the height of rough opening. Cut top and bottom panels 1/2" shorter than the width of rough opening. Cut shelves 1 1/2" shorter than the width of the opening.

(continued next page)

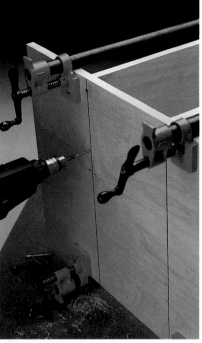

7 Attach drawer slide tracks to the center of the bottom panel and the shelves (pages 42 to 44), following manufacturer's directions.

8 Clamp and glue the shelves to the side panels to form butt joints (pages 31 to 32). Reinforce the joints with 2" screws driven through the side panels and into the edges of shelves.

9 Clamp and glue the top and bottom panels to the side panels, then reinforce the joints with 2" screws.

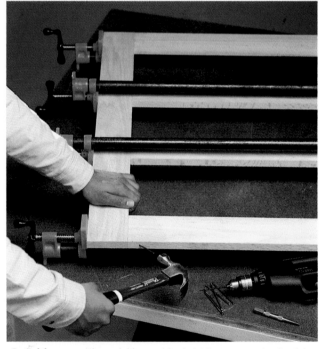

10 Measure and cut 1/4" plywood panel to cover the back of the cabinet. Attach with 1" screws or wire nails driven through the back and into the side, top, and bottom panels. To allow for expansion and contraction of wood, do not use wood glue on this joint.

11 Measure the width and height between the inside edges of the cabinet. Cut the rails to the width. Cut the stiles to the height plus 7". Clamp and glue rails between stiles, and reinforce joints by toenailing 3" finish nails through the rails and into the stiles.

12 Apply glue to edges of cabinet, then position face frame over cabinet so inside edges of the face frame are flush with the top, bottom, and side panels. Attach the face frame by drilling pilot holes and driving 1½" finish nails into the cabinet every 8". Use a nail set to countersink the nail heads.

13 Slide the cabinet into the opening so it rests on the pedestals and the face frame is against the wall surface.

14 Anchor the cabinet by drilling pilot holes and driving 3" finish nails through the face frame and into the wall framing members. Also, drive 3" finish nails through the bottom of the cabinet and into the sill.

15 Sand and finish the cabinet face frame (pages 46 to 49), then build, finish, and install overlay drawers (pages 42 to 45).

See page 15 for more utility shelf ideas

Building Utility Shelves

You can build adjustable utility shelves in a single afternoon using 2 × 4s and plain 3/4" plywood. Perfect for use in a garage or basement, utility shelves can be modified by adding side panels and a face frame to create a finished look suitable for a family room or recreation area.

The quick-and-easy shelf project shown on the following pages creates two columns of shelves with a total width of 68". You can enlarge the project easily by adding more 2 × 4 risers and plywood shelves (do not increase the individual shelf widths to more than 36"). The sole plates for the utility shelves are installed perpendicular to the wall to improve access to the space under the bottom shelves.

Everything You Need:

Tools: pencil, tape measure, level, framing square, power screwdriver, plumb bob, stud gun (concrete floors only), clamps, router with 3/4" straight bit, circular saw, stepladder.

Materials: wood glue, shims, power-driver screws (2¹/2", 3"), finishing materials.

64

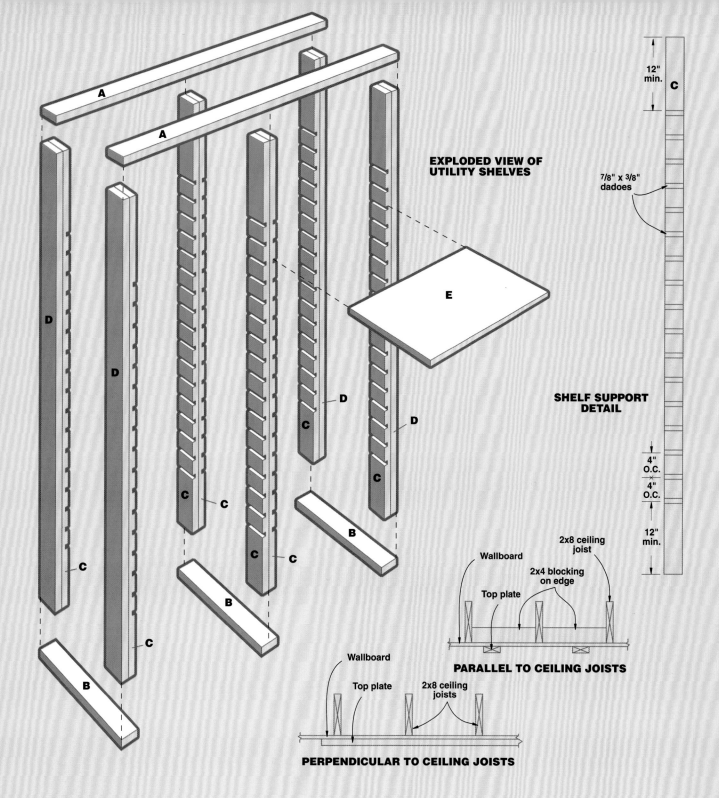

EXPLODED VIEW OF UTILITY SHELVES

12" min. C

7/8" x 3/8" dadoes

SHELF SUPPORT DETAIL

4" O.C.
4" O.C.

12" min.

Wallboard

Top plate

2x4 blocking on edge

2x8 ceiling joist

PARALLEL TO CEILING JOISTS

Wallboard

Top plate

2x8 ceiling joists

PERPENDICULAR TO CEILING JOISTS

Parts List: Utility Shelves

| Key | Part | Project as Shown | | | Your Project | |
		Material	Pieces	Size	Pieces	Size
A	Top plates	2 × 4s	2	68"		
B	Sole plates	2 × 4s	3	24"		
C	Shelf risers	2 × 4s	8	93"		
D	End risers	2 × 4s	4	93"		
E	Shelves	3/4" plywood	12	30³/4" × 24"		

How to Build Utility Shelves

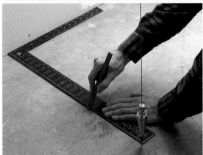

1 Mark location of top plates on ceiling. One plate should be flush against wall, and the other should be parallel to first plate, with front edge 24" from the wall. Cut 2 × 4 top plates to full length of utility shelves, then attach to ceiling joists or blocking (page 29), using 3" screws.

2 Mark points directly beneath outside corners of the top plates to find outer sole plate locations, using a plumb bob as a guide (top). Mark sole plate locations by drawing lines perpendicular to the wall connecting each pair of points (bottom).

3 Cut outer 2 × 4 sole plates and position them perpendicular to the wall, just inside the outlines. Shim plates to level if needed, then attach to floor with a stud gun or 3" screws. Attach a center sole plate midway between the outer sole plates.

4 Prepare the shelf risers by cutting 7/8"-wide, 3/4"-deep dadoes with a router. Cut dadoes every 4" along the inside face of each 2 × 4 riser, with the top and bottom dadoes cut about 12" from the ends of the 2 × 4. **TIP:** Gang-cut the risers by laying them flat and clamping them together, then attaching a straightedge guide (page 23) to align the dado cuts. For each cut, make several passes with the router, gradually extending the bit depth until dadoes are 3/4" deep.

5 Trim the shelf risers to uniform length before unclamping them. Use a circular saw and a straightedge guide.

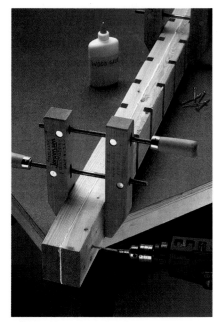  

6 Build two center shelf supports by positioning pairs of shelf risers back-to-back and joining them with wood glue and 2¹/2" screws.

7 Build four end shelf supports by positioning the back of a dadoed shelf riser against a 2 × 4 of the same length, then joining the 2 × 4 and the riser with glue and 2¹/2" screws.

8 Position an end shelf support at each corner of the shelving unit, between top and sole plates. Attach the supports by driving 3" screws "toenail" style into the top plate and sole plates.

9 Position a center shelf support (both faces dadoed) at each end of the center sole plate, then anchor shelf supports to the sole plate using 3" screws driven "toenail" style. Use a framing square to align the center shelf supports perpendicular to the top plates, then anchor to top plates.

10 Measure distance between facing dado grooves, subtract ¹/4", then cut plywood shelves to fit. Slide the shelves into the grooves.

Building Floor-to-Ceiling Shelves

Floor-to-ceiling shelves are sturdier and make better use of space than freestanding bookcases. When finished and trimmed to match the surrounding room, floor-to-ceiling shelves turn an ordinary room into an inviting den or library.

This project uses finish-grade oak plywood and a solid oak face frame to give this project the look of an expensive, solid oak shelf unit—but at a fraction of the cost. The plywood panels are supported and strengthened by an internal framework of 2 × 4 stud lumber.

When installing floor-to-ceiling shelves in a corner, as shown here, add 1/2" plywood spacers to the support studs that adjoin the wall. Spacers ensure that face frame stiles of equal width can be installed at both shelf ends (see diagram, page opposite).

Everything You Need:

Tools: tape measure, pencil, level, framing square, plumb bob, drill, hammer, circular saw, router, 3/4" straight bit.

Materials: shims, power-driver screws (13/4", 2", 3"), finish nails (11/2", 2"), metal shelf standards and clips, finishing materials, door and drawer hardware, 1/2" plywood scraps.

See page 10 for more project ideas

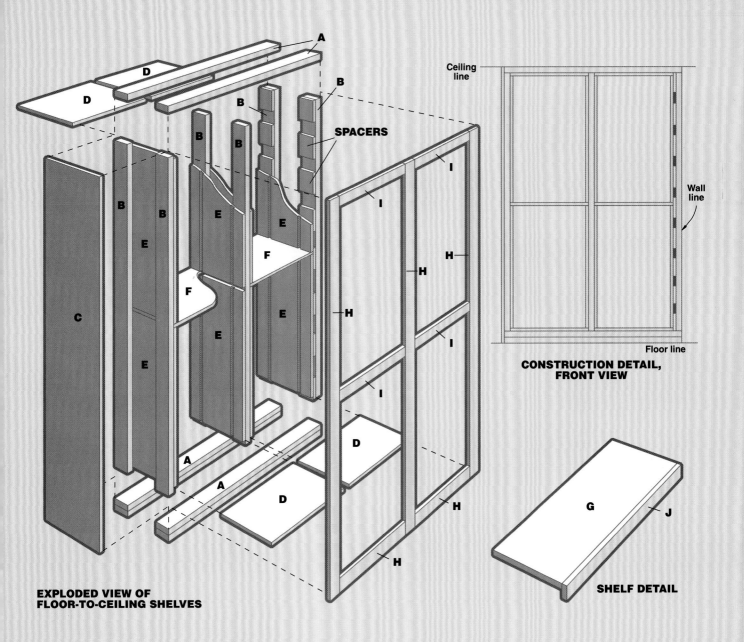

**EXPLODED VIEW OF
FLOOR-TO-CEILING SHELVES**

**CONSTRUCTION DETAIL,
FRONT VIEW**

SHELF DETAIL

SPACERS

Ceiling line

Wall line

Floor line

Parts List: Floor-to-Ceiling Shelves

		Project as Shown			Your Project	
Key	**Part**	**Material**	**Pieces**	**Size**	**Pieces**	**Size**
A	Top and sole plates	2 × 4s	6	59$\frac{1}{2}$"		
B	Support studs	2 × 4s	6	91$\frac{1}{2}$"		
C	End panel	$\frac{1}{2}$" oak plywood	1	95$\frac{3}{4}$" × 13"		
D	Top, bottom panels	$\frac{1}{2}$" oak plywood	4	27$\frac{1}{4}$" × 13"		
E	Risers	$\frac{1}{2}$" oak plywood	8	44$\frac{7}{8}$" × 13"		
F	Permanent shelves	$\frac{3}{4}$" oak plywood	2	27$\frac{1}{4}$" × 13"		
G	Adjustable shelves	$\frac{3}{4}$" oak plywood	8	26$\frac{1}{8}$" × 11$\frac{7}{8}$"		
H	Stiles and bottom rail	1 × 4 oak	28 linear ft.			
I	Top rail, middle rail	1 × 3 oak	10 linear ft.			
J	Shelf edging	1 × 2 oak	18 linear ft.			

How to Build Floor-to-Ceiling Shelves

1 Mark the location for two parallel 2 × 4 top plates on the ceiling, using a framing square as a guide. The front edge of the outer top plate should be 13" from back wall, and the other top plate should be flush against the wall. Mark location of ceiling joists; if necessary, install blocking between joists (page 29) to provide a surface for anchoring the top plates.

2 Measure and cut 2 × 4 top plates. Position each plate, check to make sure it is level, and shim if necessary. Attach plates to ceiling with 3" screws driven into the joists or blocking.

3 Cut 2 × 4 sole plates and screw them together to form two doubled sole plates. Use a plumb bob suspended from the outside corners of the top plates to align the sole plates, then shim to level, if needed; anchor the plates by driving 3" screws toenail-style into the floor.

4 Install 2 × 4 support studs between the ends of the top plates and sole plates. Attach support studs with 3" screws driven toenail-style into the top plates and sole plates.

5 Install center support studs midway between the end support studs. Attach to bottom plate first, using 3" screws driven toenail-style. Use a level to make sure that stud is plumb, then attach the studs to the top plate with 3" screws.

6 Where the shelves fit into a corner, use 2" screws to attach 1/2" plywood spacers on the inside faces of the support studs, spaced every 4". Make sure spacers do not extend past the front face of the studs.

7 Where the end of the project is exposed, measure and cut a 1/2" plywood end panel to floor-to-ceiling height. Attach the panel to the support studs so the front edges are flush, using 13/4" screws driven through the support studs and into the end panel.

8 Measure and cut 1/2" plywood top and bottom panels to fit between the support studs. Attach to the top and sole plates using 11/2" finish nails.

9 Measure and cut lower risers from 1/2" plywood, then cut dadoes for metal shelf standards (page 37).

10 Install lower risers on each side of the 2 × 4 support studs so the front edges are flush with the edges of the studs. Attach risers with 11/2" finish nails driven into the support studs. For riser that adjoins wall, drive nails at spacer locations.

11 Measure and cut permanent shelves from 3/4" plywood to fit between the support studs, just above the lower risers. Set shelves on risers and attach them with 11/2" finish nails driven down into the risers.

(continued next page)

12 Measure and cut upper risers to fit between the permanent shelves and the top panels. Cut dadoes for metal shelf standards, then attach the risers to the support studs with 1$\frac{1}{2}$" finish nails.

13 Measure and cut 1 × 3 stiles to reach from floor to ceiling along the front edges of the exposed support studs. Drill pilot holes and attach the stiles to the support studs so they are flush with the risers, using glue and 1$\frac{1}{2}$" finish nails driven at 8" intervals into the studs and risers.

14 Measure and cut 1 × 3 top rails to fit between the stiles. Drill pilot holes and attach the rails to the top plate and top panels, using glue and 1$\frac{1}{2}$" finish nails.

15 Measure and cut 1 × 4 bottom rails to fit between the stiles. Drill pilot holes, and attach the rails to the sole plates and bottom panels, using glue and 1$\frac{1}{2}$" finish nails. The top edge of the rails should be flush with the top surface of the plywood panels.

16 Fill nail holes, then sand and finish the wood surfaces (pages 46 to 49).

17 Measure, cut, and install metal shelf standards into the dadoes (page 37), using nails or screws provided by the manufacturer.

18 Measure and cut adjustable shelves 1/8" shorter than the distance between metal standards. Cut shelf edging, and attach with glue and 1 1/2" finish nails. Sand and finish the shelves.

19 Insert shelf clips into metal shelf standards and install the adjustable shelves at desired heights.

20 Cover gaps between the project and walls and floor with molding that has been finished to match the shelf unit.

See page 11 for more platform bench ideas

Building a Platform Bench

A platform bench combines convenient storage with a generous seating area. Because of its low profile and adaptability, a platform bench fits nicely into many locations: next to a built-in bookcase, in a window bay, or along a flat wall beneath a picture window. When used as a window seat, a platform bench is a perfect spot for relaxing on a sunny morning. Cushions and throw pillows soften the look and feel of the bench. And when aromatic cedar panels are added, the interior of the built-in becomes an ideal storage space for quilts and fine linens.

The platform bench shown here is 21" high, 24" deep, and 48" long. With careful cutting, the main panels of the project may be cut from a single 4 ft. × 8 ft. sheet of oak plywood. By raising or lowering the height of the side panels, you can adapt the design to any height you find comfortable, though you may need additional plywood.

If you build a platform bench more than 48" long, add a vertical face frame stile in the center of the opening for extra support.

Everything You Need:

Tools: tape measure, level, pencil, power screwdriver, drill, circular saw, wood chisel, hammer, nail set, clamps, dowel jig.

Materials: shims, finish nails (1", 2"), power-driver screws (1/2", 2", 2 1/2", 3"), fluted dowels, glue, aromatic cedar panels, semi-concealed hinges, door catches, finishing materials, wood plugs, corner brackets, door hardware.

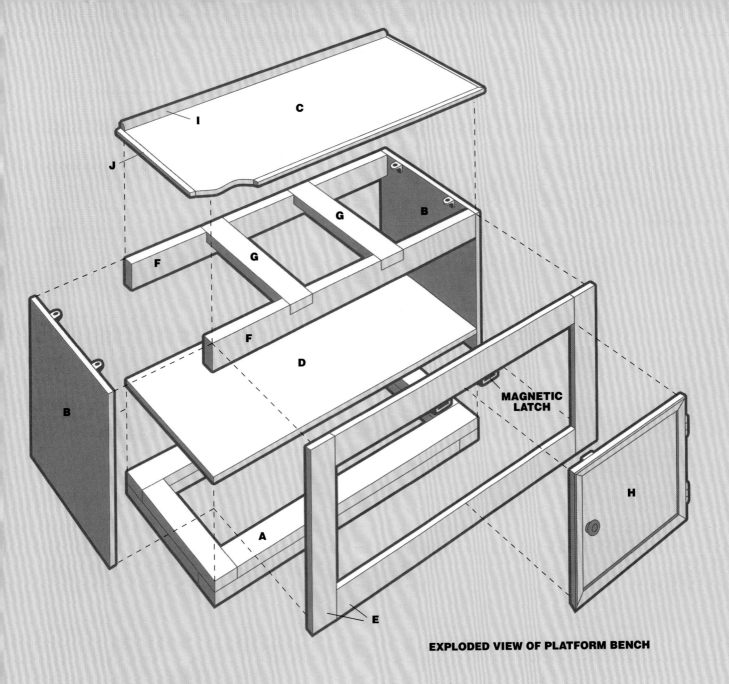

EXPLODED VIEW OF PLATFORM BENCH

MAGNETIC LATCH

Parts List: Platform Bench

Project as Shown					Your Project	
Key	Part	Material	Pieces	Size	Pieces	Size
A	Pedestals	2 × 4s	2	46$\frac{1}{2}$" × 24"		
B	Side panels	3/4" oak plywood	2	24" × 21"		
C	Top panel (seat)	3/4" oak plywood	1	48" × 24$\frac{3}{4}$"		
D	Bottom panel	3/4" oak plywood	1	46$\frac{1}{2}$" × 24"		
E	Face frame	1 × 4 oak	12 linear ft.			
F	Supports	2 × 4	2	46$\frac{1}{2}$"		
G	Cross braces	2 × 4	2	24"		
H	Overlay doors		see pages 38 to 41			
I	Trim	Base shoe molding	12 linear ft.			
J	Top panel edging	Shelf-edge molding	7 linear ft.			

Platform Bench Project Details

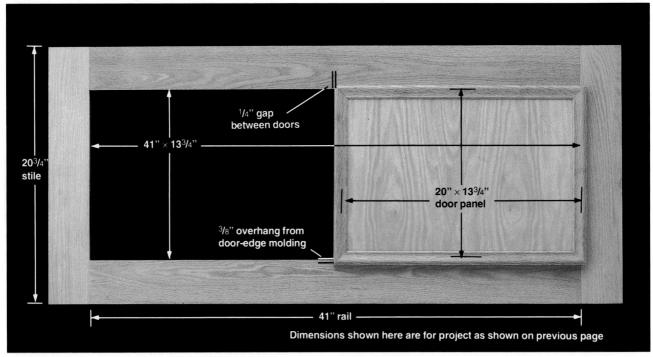

20³/₄" stile

41" × 13³/₄"

¹/₄" gap between doors

20" × 13³/₄" door panel

³/₈" overhang from door-edge molding

41" rail

Dimensions shown here are for project as shown on previous page

Face frame for the platform bench shown on the previous page is built with 1 × 4 oak stiles and rails joined with blind dowel joints (pages 34 to 35) and installed as one piece. For a good fit, measure and build the face frame after the cabinet is assembled.

Door panels are made from ¹/₂" finish-grade plywood and door-edge molding (pages 38 to 41). The panels overlap the face frame by ³/₈", and they are sized to leave a ¹/₄" gap between the doors. Hang the doors with semi-concealed hinges.

How to Build a Platform Bench

1 Measure and mark a level reference line where the top of the platform bench will fit against the wall. Benches installed below a window should be centered with the window.

2 Build a pedestal base from a double layer of 2 × 4s, laid flat and joined together with 2¹/₂" screws. For greatest pedestal strength, stagger the ends of the 2 × 4s.

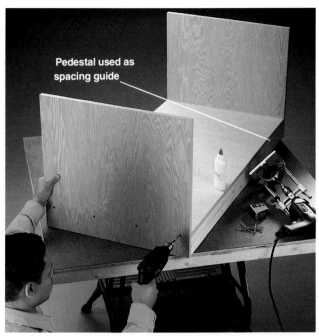

Pedestal used as spacing guide

3 Measure and cut a bottom panel (same size as pedestal) and side panels (planned height minus 3/4" for top panel). Rest the bottom panel on the pedestal to achieve proper spacing, then attach the side panels to the base panel, using glue and 2 1/2" screws driven through counterbored pilot holes, at 6" intervals. Do not attach panels to pedestal.

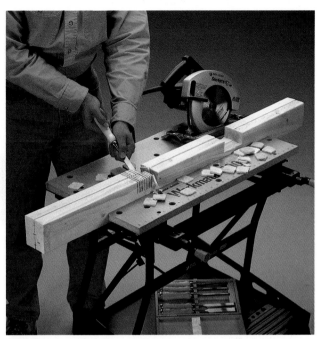

4 Measure and cut two 2 × 4 supports to the same length as the bottom panel, then clamp the supports together on your workbench, with ends aligned. Cut 1 1/2"-deep, 3 1/2"-wide notches in each 2 × 4, 14" in from each end. Cut notches by making multiple passes using a circular saw with blade set to 1 1/2", then removing the waste wood with a wood chisel.

5 Position the supports at the front and back of the bench cabinet, flush with the tops and sides of the side panels. Drill counterbored pilot holes in the side panels, then attach the supports with glue and 2 1/2" screws.

Supports

Cross braces

6 Cut 2 × 4 cross braces the same depth as the base panel. Apply glue to the notches on the supports, then insert the cross braces into the notches and secure them with 2 1/2" screws.

(continued next page)

7 Set the pedestal in the planned location, check to make sure it is level, and shim between the pedestal and the floor if necessary. Anchor the pedestal with 3" screws driven toenail-style into the floor and at shim locations, from inside the pedestal. Trim off shim ends.

8 Set the bench cabinet onto the pedestal, flush against the wall.

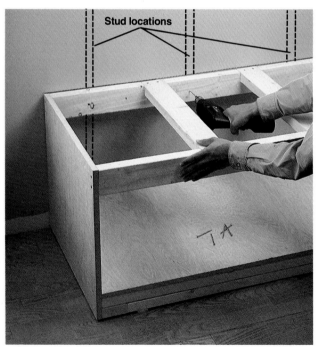

9 Attach the back support of the bench cabinet to the wall with 3" screws driven at wall stud locations, then anchor the bench cabinet to the pedestal by driving 2" screws down through the bottom panel.

10 Measure exact height and length of cabinet and pedestal, then cut 1 × 4 hardwood stiles for face frame, 1/4" shorter than bench height. Cut 1 × 4 rails for face frame, 7" shorter than bench length. Assemble the face frame using blind dowel joints (pages 34 to 35).

11 Attach the face frame to the front edges of the bench cabinet, using 2" finish nails and glue. The top edge of the bottom face frame rail should be flush with the surface of the bottom panel, leaving a gap above the floor.

12 Build two overlay doors to fit the face frame opening (pages 38 to 41). When determining the size of the door panels, allow for a 1/4" gap between the doors after door-edge molding is attached.

13 Attach the doors to the face frame using semi-concealed hinges.

14 Attach magnetic door catches to the top rail of the face frame and to doors, following the manufacturer's directions.

(continued next page)

15 Attach aromatic cedar panels to the inside surfaces of the bench cabinet, or stain and varnish the interior of the cabinet (pages 46 to 49), before attaching the top panel.

16 Attach two corner brackets (for anchoring top panel) to the inside face of each side panel, flush with the top edges.

17 Measure and cut a 3/4" oak plywood top panel to fit against the wall and flush with the outside edges of the face frame. Set the top panel in position on the bench cabinet, and attach it from below by driving 1/2" screws through the corner brackets. Drive 2" screws through the 2 × 4 cross braces and into the underside of the top panel.

18 Cover the exposed edges of the top panel with mitered shelf-edge molding. Attach the molding pieces with glue and 1" finish nails driven every 4" to 6" through pilot holes.

19 Cover gaps between platform bench and floor with mitered base shoe molding, attached with glue and 1" finish nails driven through pilot holes.

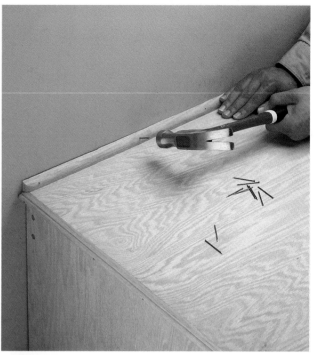

20 Cover gaps between platform bench and wall with base shoe molding, attached with glue and 1" finish nails driven through pilot holes.

21 Countersink finish nails with a nail set, and fill all nail and screw holes. Sand and finish the platform bench (pages 46 to 49), then attach door pulls.

See page 13 for more corner cabinet ideas

A desktop and computer desk accessories transform this corner cabinet into a handsome, functional work center. A retractable keyboard shelf supports the keyboard at an easy working height. Computer cables are kept out of sight and tangle-free by a wire organizer. An outlet strip mounted on the desktop is easy to reach and protects the computer from power surges. See pages 50 to 51 for information on electrical accessories.

Building a Corner Cabinet

Most furniture sold in stores does not fit well in a corner. But due to its triangular shape and efficient design, a built-in corner cabinet fits naturally into any room corner.

The corner cabinet featured here includes side panels that make the cabinet deeper. Installed at a right angle to the wall, the side panels also create a good surface for attaching a built-in bookcase.

The corner cabinet as shown was created using dimensions and angles that fit almost any corner, and allow for many uses. For this reason, altering the design is unnecessary and not recommended.

Most tasks in the corner cabinet project can be done with everyday tools, but the long bevel cuts needed for the face frame and side panels are best done with a table saw. If you do not own a table saw, either rent one, or have the cuts made at a woodworking shop.

Due to its size and weight, a corner cabinet should be assembled on-site.

Everything You Need:

Tools: pencil, straightedge, level, handscrew clamps, drill and bits, hammer, jig saw, table saw, utility knife.

Materials: wood glue, finish nails (1", 1 1/2", 2"), power-driver screws (1 1/4", 1 1/2", 2", 3"), 3/4" wire nails, shims, computer desk accessories (photo left, and pages 50 to 51), base shoe molding.

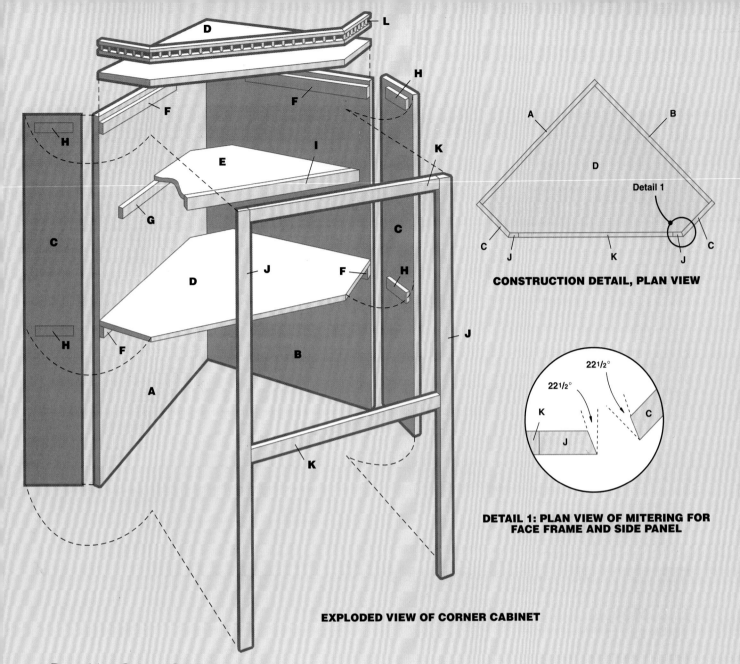

CONSTRUCTION DETAIL, PLAN VIEW

**DETAIL 1: PLAN VIEW OF MITERING FOR
FACE FRAME AND SIDE PANEL**

EXPLODED VIEW OF CORNER CABINET

Parts List: Corner Cabinet

Key	Part	Material	Pieces	Size
A	Left back panel	3/4" oak plywood	1	39" × 66"
B	Right back panel	3/4" oak plywood	1	38 1/4" × 66"
C	Side panels	3/4" oak plywood	2	10" × 66"
D	Desktop and top panel	3/4" oak plywood	2	38 1/4" × 38 1/4" (see detail, page 84)
E	Shelf	3/4" oak plywood	1	34" × 34" (see detail, page 84)
F	Cleats for desktop, top panel	1 × 2	4	31"
G	Cleats for shelf	1 × 2	2	27"
H	Cleats on side panels	1 × 2	4	6"
I	Shelf edging	1 × 2	1	51 1/2"
J	Face frame stiles	1 × 2	2	66"
K	Face frame rails	1 × 2	2	37 1/2"
L	Decorative top trim	spindle rail		5 linear ft.

Corner Cabinet Project Details

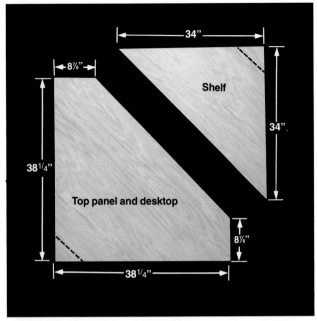

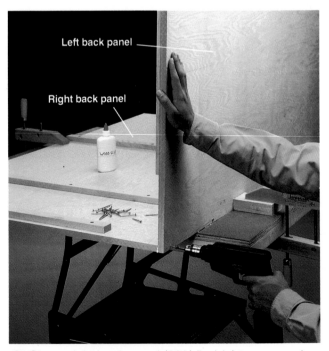

Desktop, top panel, and shelf are made from 3/4" finish-grade plywood. Use a circular saw and a straightedge guide to cut the pieces to the dimensions shown above. If you plan to use the cabinet as a computer work center or an entertainment center, cut off the back corners of the desktop and shelf (but not the top panel) to provide ventilation and space for routing electrical cords.

Back panel and side panels have 1 × 2 hardwood cleats to hold the desktop, shelf, and top panel. Attach them to the panels with glue and 1½" screws driven into counterbored pilot holes. Position cleats according to dimensions shown above. **NOTE:** If you wish to make the shelf the same size as the desktop, add shelf cleats to the side panels (dotted line).

How to Build a Corner Cabinet

1 Measure and cut back panels (left panel overlaps right panel, so it is 3/4" wider than right panel). Cut and attach 1 × 2 cleats according to Project Details (above). Drill counterbored pilot holes in cleats, then attach cleats with glue and 1¼" screws.

2 Clamp right back panel (38¼" wide) to your workbench, then apply glue to back edge. Butt left panel (39") against glued edge, and hold in place with clamps. Join back panels by drilling pilot holes and driving 2" screws through butt joint.

3 Attach a plastic wire organizer to one back panel edge, next to the corner joint, using 1" wire nails. (Skip this step if you do not plan to store electronic equipment in the corner cabinet.)

4 Measure and cut the desktop (see Project Details, page opposite), then apply glue to the tops of the desktop cleats mounted on the back panels. Set the desktop on the cleats, then attach by drilling pilot holes and driving 1¹/4" finish nails every 8".

5 Measure and cut shelf (see Project Details), then install on shelf cleats with glue and 1¹/4" finish nails. Measure and cut a 1 × 2 hardwood shelf edge with 45° mitered corners to fit flush with top of shelf. Attach with 2" finish nails driven through pilot holes.

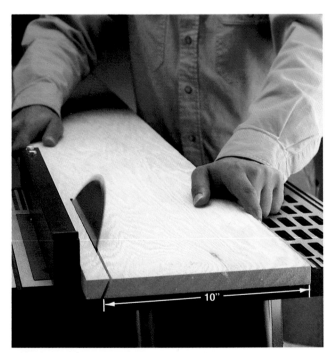

6 Set a table saw blade to 22¹/2° blade angle, then cut 10"-wide, 66"-long side panels, beveling the front edge of each panel.

7 Attach 6" cleats to side panels (see Project Details) using glue and 1¹/4" finish nails, then attach side panels to back panels with glue and 1¹/2" screws driven into counterbored pilot holes. Cut top panel (see Project Details) and attach to cleats with 1¹/4" finish nails.

(continued next page)

8 With table saw blade set to 22½°, cut 1 × 2 face frame stiles (as in step 6). Apply glue to the outside edge of each side panel, then attach stiles to side panels using 2" finish nails driven through pilot holes at 8" intervals.

9 Measure and cut 1 × 2 face frame rails. Attach them to edges of desktop and top panel, so upper edges of rails are flush with the surfaces of the shelf and top, using glue and 2" finish nails driven through pilot holes.

10 Measure and cut decorative trim to match the angle of the face frame stiles and side panels, then attach the trim to the outside edges at the top of the cabinet, using finish nails.

11 With a helper, move cabinet into corner, flush against the walls.

12 Shim below the side panels, if necessary, to bring the cabinet to level.

13 Drill pilot holes, then toenail the cabinet to the floor at shim locations, using 2" finish nails. Score the shims with a utility knife, then break off the excess shim material.

14 Attach the cabinet to the wall with 3" screws driven through the back panels and into wall studs. Drive screws just behind or below shelf cleats to keep them out of sight.

15 Measure and cut base shoe molding to cover the gap between the cabinet and the walls and floor, using 1 1/2" finish nails. **TIP:** To protect wall from oil or paint, insert plastic between molding and wall as you attach the molding.

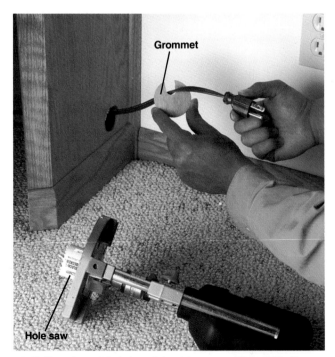

Grommet

Hole saw

16 Sand and finish cabinet (pages 46 to 49), then remove plastic. If cabinet will contain electronic equipment, use a hole saw or forstner bit to cut a hole for an outlet strip cord in side panel, then feed cord through hole and install a grommet (page 51).

17 Install any other hardware and computer desk accessories, like a retractable keyboard slide, that you need to complete your project (see manufacturer's directions and pages 50 to 51).

Building Basic Cabinets

The simple base cabinet and hanging wall cabinet shown here use the same basic construction as professionally built kitchen cabinets, but because they are custom-designed, trimmed, and finished to blend into the room, they become permanent built-in features of your home.

These basic cabinets are built with oak plywood, which gives them the look of fine custom-made cabinets, but at a much reduced cost. The wall cabinet features glass-panel doors, purchased separately, that create an ideal display area for glassware or china. The base cabinet has extra-large drawers that are well suited for storing table linens.

You can use the methods shown here to build a single base cabinet with a wall cabinet above it, or several cabinets side by side (for a full wall of storage or display).

Everything You Need:

Tools: electronic stud finder, cordless screwdriver, hammer, tape measure, router with bits (3/4" straight, 1/4" rabbet), drill and bits, right-angle drill guide, pegboard scraps, pipe clamps, level.

Materials: power-driver screws (3/4", 21/2", 31/2"), wood glue, finish nails (1", 2", 3", 4"), shims, utility knife, pin-style shelf supports, 2 × 4 brace, 1 × 3 for ledger strip, finishing materials, drawer and door hardware, trim or base shoe molding.

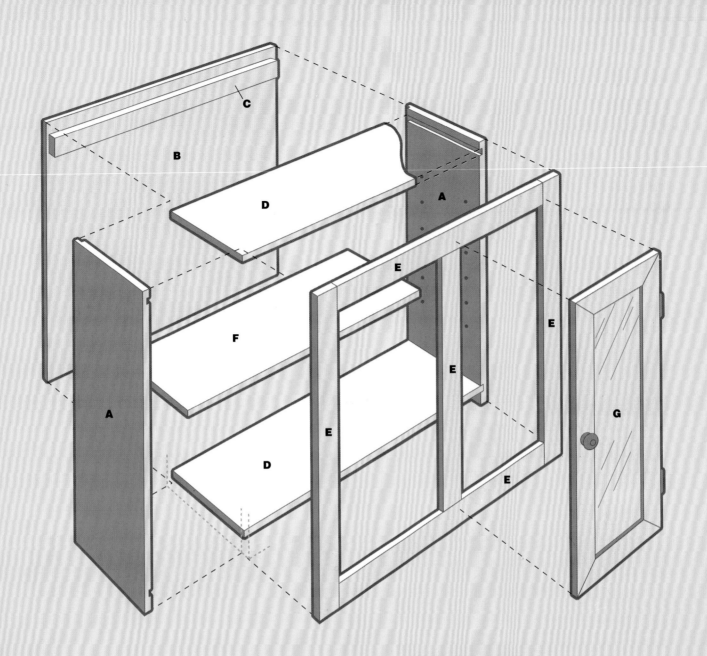

**EXPLODED VIEW OF
HANGING WALL CABINET**

Parts List: Wall Cabinet

	Project as Shown				Your Project	
Key	**Part**	**Material**	**Pieces**	**Size**	**Pieces**	**Size**
A	Side panels	3/4" oak plywood	2	11¼" × 30"		
B	Back panel	1/4" oak plywood	1	30" × 35¼"		
C	Nailing strip	1 × 3 oak	1	34¼"		
D	Top, bottom panels	3/4" oak plywood	2	35¼" × 11¼"		
E	Face frame	1 × 3 oak	12 linear ft.			
F	Shelves	3/4" oak plywood	2	9¾" × 34¼"		
G	Glass panel or overlay doors		pages 40 to 41			

Wall Cabinet Project Details

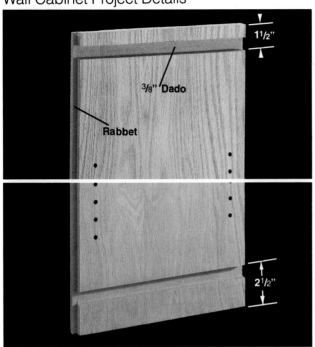

Side panels made from 3/4" plywood have 3/4"-wide, 3/8"-deep dadoes where bottom and top panels will fit and 1/4" wide rabbets where back panel will fit. Rows of parallel peg holes, 11/2" in from edges, will hold pin-style shelf supports.

Back panel made from 1/4" plywood has a 1 × 3 nailing strip mounted 11/2" below top edge of the back panel and set in 3/8" on each side. It is fastened with glue and 3/4" screws driven through the back panel.

How to Build & Install a Wall Cabinet

1 Measure and cut 3/4" plywood side panels, then cut rabbets and dadoes, using a router and a straightedge guide (page 23), following the dimensions in the Project Details (above).

2 Drill two parallel rows of 1/4" holes for pin-style shelf supports on the inside face of each side panel (page 38). Use a right-angle drill guide, and a scrap of pegboard as a template to ensure that holes line up correctly.

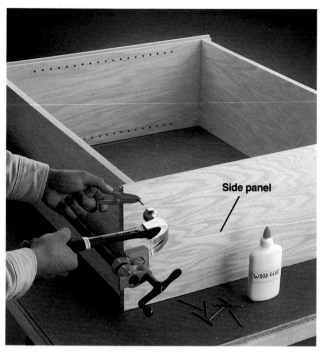

3 Measure and cut 3/4" plywood top and bottom panels, then glue and clamp the side panels to the top and bottom panels to form dado joints (page 33). Reinforce the joints with 2" finish nails driven every 3".

4 Measure, cut, and attach 1 × 3 nailing strip to the back panel (see Project Details), using glue and 3/4" screws. Set the back panel into the rabbets at the back edges of the cabinet. Secure the back with 11/2" wire nails driven into the cabinet edges.

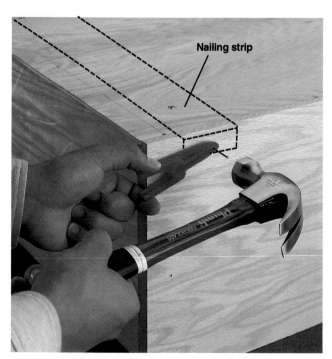

5 Drive 2" finish nails through the side panel and into the ends of the nailing strip.

6 Measure height and width between inside surfaces of cabinet, then cut 1 × 3 face frame rails 43/4" less than the width, and face frame stiles 4" longer than height. Clamp and glue rails between stiles, and reinforce joints by drilling pilot holes and driving 4" finish nails through the stiles into the rails.

(continued next page)

7 Center the face frame on the cabinet so overhang on each side is equal, and top edge of the bottom rail is flush with bottom shelf surface. Attach the face frame with glue and 2" finish nails driven through pilot holes.

8 Fill nail holes, then sand and finish the cabinet (pages 46 to 49).

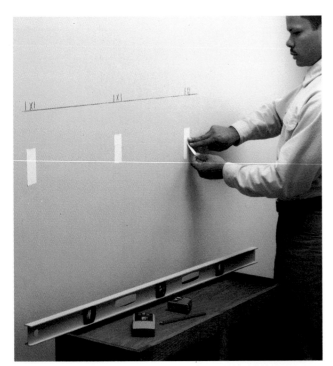

9 Mark a level reference line on the wall where the bottom edge of the cabinet will be located— 54" above the floor is a standard height. Locate the wall studs, and mark their location below the reference line.

10 Position a temporary 1 × 3 ledger strip so top edge is flush with the reference line, then attach the strip to the wall at stud locations, using 2 1/2" screws.

11 Set cabinet on the temporary ledger, and brace it in position with a 2 × 4. Drill counterbored pilot holes in the nailing strip at the top of the cabinet, and drive 3" screws into wall studs.

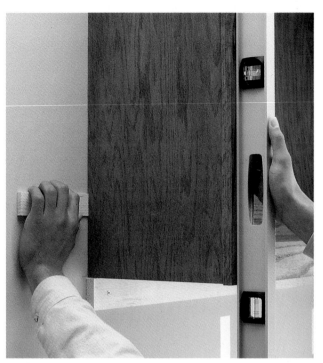

12 Use a level to make sure cabinet is plumb. If not, loosen screws slightly and shim behind the cabinet to adjust it to plumb. Tighten screws completely, then score shims with a utility knife and break off excess.

13 Remove temporary ledger and patch screw holes, then cut trim molding to cover gaps between cabinet and the walls. Drill pilot holes and attach trim with 1" finish nails.

14 Build and finish shelves with pin-style shelf supports (pages 36 to 37). Build or purchase overlay doors (pages 38 to 41), and attach them to the face frame. Sand and finish the cabinets (pages 46 to 49), then attach hardware and install shelf support pins and adjustable shelves.

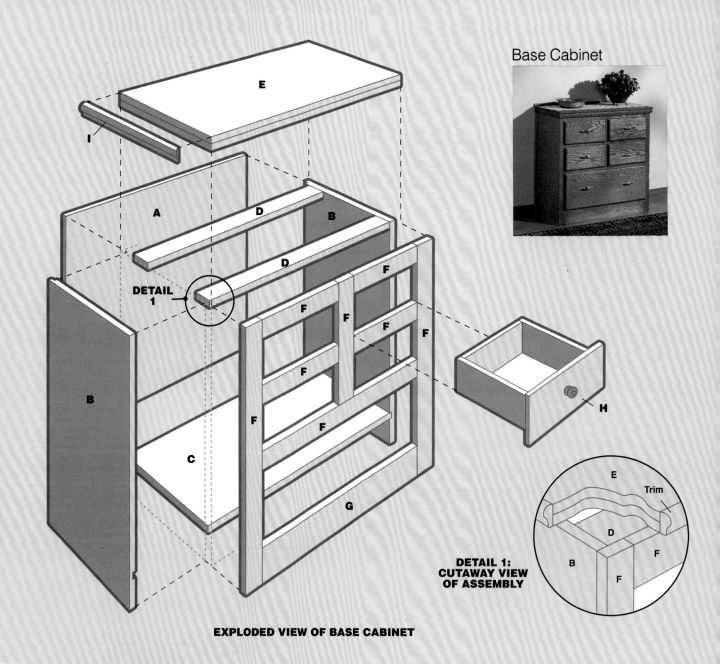

Base Cabinet

EXPLODED VIEW OF BASE CABINET

**DETAIL 1:
CUTAWAY VIEW
OF ASSEMBLY**

Parts List: Base Cabinet

Project as Shown					Your Project	
Key	**Part**	**Material**	**Pieces**	**Size**	**Pieces**	**Size**
A	Back panel	1/2" plywood	1	34 1/2" × 35 1/4"		
B	Side panels	3/4" plywood	2	34 1/2" × 17 1/4"		
C	Bottom panel	3/4" plywood	1	16 3/4" × 35 1/4"		
D	Supports	1 × 3 oak	2	34 1/2"		
E	Countertop	3/4" plywood	2	36 1/4"× 18"		
F	Face frame	1 × 3 oak	15 linear ft.			
G	Bottom rail	1 × 6 oak	1	31 1/4 "		
H	Overlay drawers	pages 42 to 45				
I	Trim molding	12 linear ft.				

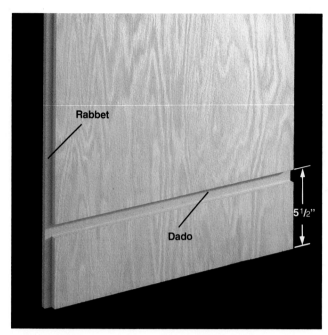

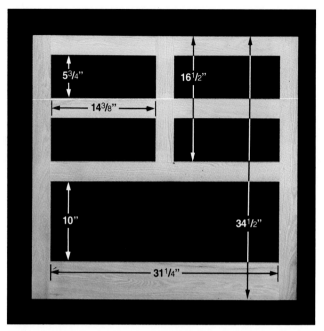

Side panels made from ³/4" plywood have ³/4"-wide, ³/8"-deep dadoes to hold bottom panel, and ¹/2"-wide, ³/8"-deep rabbets where back panel will fit. Bottom dado is raised so bottom drawer will be at a comfortable height.

Face frame includes 1 × 6 bottom rails, and 1 × 3s for the stiles and other rails. Cut and assemble face frame, following dimensions shown in photo above.

How to Build & Install a Base Cabinet

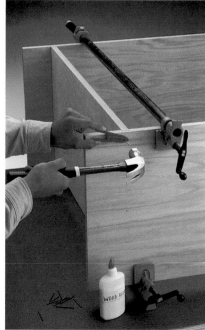

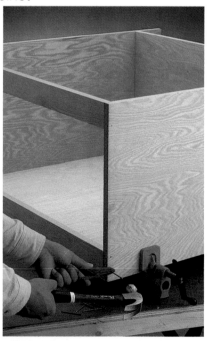

1 Cut ³/4" plywood side and bottom panels, and ¹/2" plywood back panel. Cut rabbets and dadoes, following Project Details (above), and assemble the pieces with glue and 2" finish nails, following steps 1 through 4, pages 98 to 99.

2 Measure, cut, and install two 1 × 3 supports to fit between the side panels at the top of the cabinet. Attach with 2" finish nails driven through the side panels.

3 Measure, cut, and assemble face frame following Project Detail (above), and steps 6 to 7, pages 91 to 92.

(continued next page)

4 Mark location of wall studs in project area, then set cabinet in place. Check with a level and shim under cabinet, if necessary to level it. Toenail the side panels to the floor at shim locations, using 2" finish nails. Score shims, and break off excess.

5 Anchor the cabinet by driving 3½" screws through the back panel and into wall studs just below the top of the cabinet.

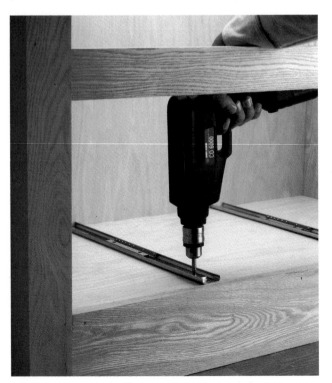

6 Install tracks for two center-mounted drawer slides on the bottom panel (pages 42 to 45).

7 Attach drawer slides for upper drawers to the face frame rails and the back panel, following the manufacturer's directions.

8 Measure and cut two 3/4" plywood countertop panels. Fasten them together with glue and 1" screws driven up through the bottom layer. Set countertop on cabinet, and anchor it with 2" screws driven up through the supports inside the cabinet.

9 Cover exposed edges of countertop with mitered ornamental molding, attached with glue and 2" finish nails driven through pilot holes.

10 Cover gaps between the cabinet and the walls and floor with trim molding, attached with 1" finish nails driven through pilot holes. Finish the cabinet (pages 46 to 49).

11 Build overlay drawers (pages 42 to 45), and finish them to match the cabinet. Install drawers and attach drawer pulls.

See page 14 for more
Understairs Work Center ideas

Building an Understairs Work Center

The irregular space beneath a staircase can be used for a variety of creative built-in projects. Because the dimensions and angles of understairs areas vary widely, finding stock cabinetry that fits the space is difficult. But the design shown here can be built to fit almost any area.

The understairs work center, in its simplest form, is a pair of basic cabinets that support a countertop. The basic cabinets are built to a standard height, depending on the use. You can adapt the size of the understairs work center by shortening or lengthening the countertop and connecting shelf. A small cabinet and upper shelves are added to fill out the remaining space. The depth of the countertop also can be adjusted to match the width of your staircase.

Most understairs projects require that you make many angled cuts, but in the project shown here, you will need to make only a few miters and bevels. Beveled cuts can be made with a circular saw, but a table saw is preferable.

Everything You Need:

Tools: pencil, tape measure, level, T-bevel, circular saw or table saw, cordless screwdriver, drill and bits, hammer, router with 3/4" straight bit and 3/8" rabbet bit, bar clamps, miter saw.

Materials: shims, finish nails (1", 1 1/4", 2"), power-driver screws (1", 1 1/4", 2 1/2"), 1" wire nails, trim molding, finishing materials, door and drawer hardware.

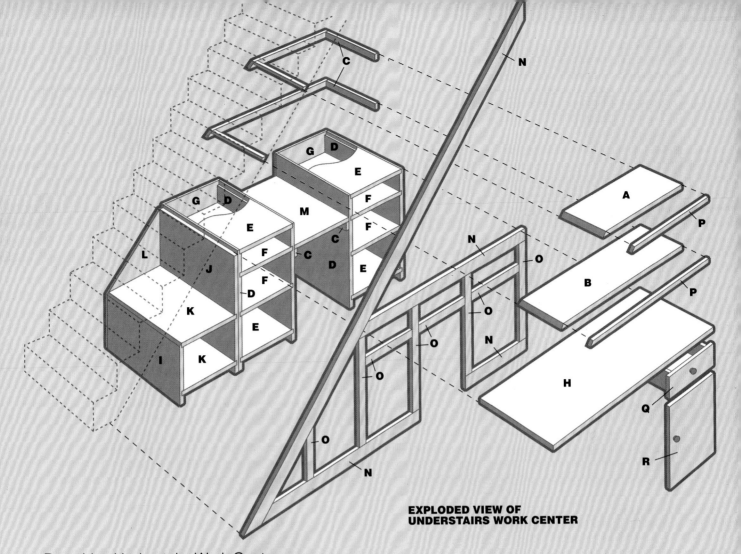

**EXPLODED VIEW OF
UNDERSTAIRS WORK CENTER**

Parts List: Understairs Work Center

Project as Shown					Your Project	
Key	Part	Material	Pieces	Size	Pieces	Size
A	Top shelf	3/4" plywood	1	28" × 18"		
B	Lower shelf	3/4" plywood	1	42" × 18"		
C	Shelf cleats	1 × 2	12 linear ft.			
D	Cabinet sides	3/4" plywood	4	35 1/2" × 24"		
E	Cabinet base, top panels	3/4" plywood	4	24" × 19 1/4"		
F	Cabinet shelves	3/4" plywood	4	24" × 19 1/4"		
G	Cabinet backs	1/4" plywood	2	20" × 35"		
H	Countertop	3/4" plywood	1	32" × 64"		
I	Small cabinet side	3/4" plywood	1	18" × 24"		
J	Small cabinet side	3/4" plywood	1	34 1/2" × 24"		
K	Small cabinet bottom & top	3/4" plywood	2	19 1/4" × 24"		
L	Small cabinet back	1/4" plywood	1	20" × 34"		
M	Connecting shelf	3/4" plywood	1	27 7/8" × 24"		
N	Face frame pieces	1 × 3 oak	26 linear ft.			
O	Face frame pieces	1 × 2 oak	25 linear ft.			
P	Shelf edge strips	3/4" hardwood	4 linear ft.			
Q	Drawers	see pages 42 to 45				
R	Cabinet doors	see pages 38 to 41				

Understudies Work Center Project Details

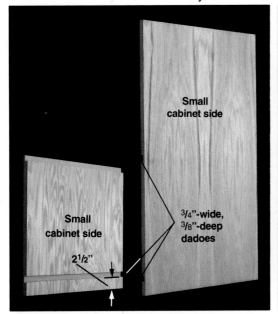

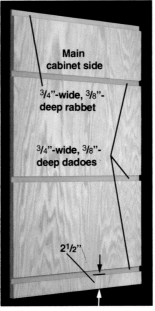

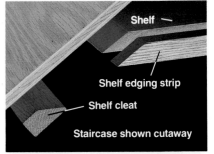

Side panels for short cabinet (left), made from 3/4" plywood, differ in size. A line connecting the tops of the two panels should follow the slope line of the staircase. **Side panels for main cabinets (right),** also made from 3/4" plywood, have dadoes for the cabinet shelves and base, and rabbets for the cabinet top. The taller side panel for the small cabinet fits against a main cabinet side panel when the work center is installed.

Shelves and cleats, made from plywood and 1 × 2 strips, are beveled so they fit flush against the understudies cover. The shelf edging strips are cut from oak 1 × 2, and mitered at the same angle as the shelves.

Tips for Building an Understudies Work Center

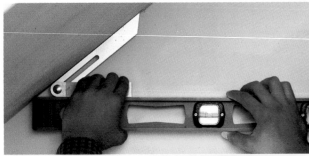

Duplicate the slope of your stairs using a T-bevel. Set one arm of the T-bevel in a level position against the back wall, then align the other arm with the stairs (top photo). Transfer the angle directly to your saw to make mitered and beveled cuts (bottom photo).

Cover stair underside before you install your understudies work center. Panels of 1/2" plywood attached to the stringers of the staircase create an understudies cover that can be used to anchor shelf cleats. If you plan to add electrical or plumbing lines, do the work (or hire a professional if you are inexperienced) before installing your built-in.

How to Build an Understairs Work Center

1 Mark the location for the shelf cleats on the walls and understairs cover, using a level as a guide. Butt the 12" cleats against the back wall, and allow at least 12" of clearance between the countertop and the bottom shelf.

2 Measure and cut 1 × 2 shelf cleats to fit along the reference lines on the walls and the understairs cover (see Project Details, page opposite). Bevel the cleats on the understairs cover to match the stair slope angle. Attach the cleats with 2½" screws.

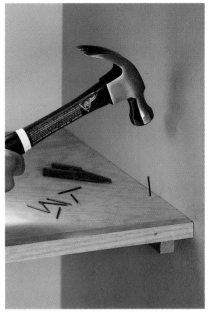

3 Measure and cut 3/4" plywood shelves, then attach a 3/4" hardwood strip to each shelf edge (see Project Details, page opposite) using glue and finish nails. Set shelves on cleats and attach with 1½" finish nails driven through pilot holes.

4 Measure and cut 3/4" plywood side panels for main cabinets, then use a router and straightedge guide (page 23) to cut rabbets for top panels and dadoes for bottom panels and shelves (see Project Details, page opposite).

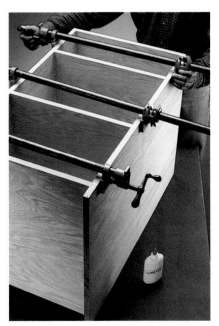

5 Clamp and glue the cabinet sides to the top and bottom panels and shelves to form rabbet and dado joints. **NOTE:** If you plan to install center-mounted drawer slides, mount slide tracks before you assemble the cabinet.

6 Reinforce each cabinet joint with 2" finish nails driven at 4" intervals.

(continued next page)

7 Cut a 1/4" plywood back panel for each main cabinet. Set each back onto a cabinet frame so all sides align, then attach to cabinet side, base, and top panels using 1" wire nails.

8 Position one cabinet so top panel is pressed against the understairs cover and front face is flush with edge of stairway. Shim if needed, then toenail into the floor through the side panels, using 2" finish nails. For masonry floors, attach with construction adhesive.

9 Position other cabinet 3/4" away from side wall, with front face aligned with first cabinet. Check with a level and shim if needed. Insert 3/4" spacers between cabinet and side wall, then anchor to wall with 2 1/2" screws driven into framing members.

10 Cut 1 × 2 cleats for the connecting shelf that fits between the main cabinets. Mark level lines on the inner cabinet sides, then attach shelf cleats to the cabinet sides by driving 1 1/4" screws through counterbored pilot holes.

11 Measure and cut a 3/4" plywood connecting shelf to fit between the cabinets, and attach it to the cleats with 1 1/4" finish nails. (If you plan to build a drawer using a center-mounted drawer slide, attach the slide track to the shelf before you attach the shelf to the cleats.)

12 Measure and cut a plywood countertop panel that extends all the way to the back wall, with one side flush against the understairs cover. Attach the countertop to top panels of cabinets by driving 1½" finish nails down through the countertop.

13 Apply or install any special countertop finishing material, like ceramic tile or plastic laminate. Obtain installation instructions and follow them carefully if you have not installed tile or laminate before.

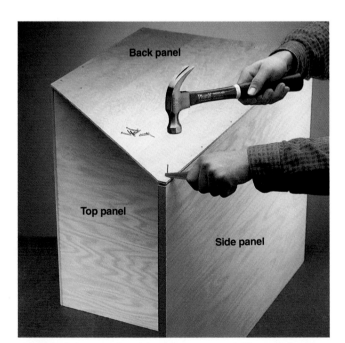

Back panel

Top panel

Side panel

14 Build a small cabinet the same width and depth as the main cabinets (steps 4 to 7). Adjust the height of the side panels to follow the stair slope (see Project Details, page 100). Cut a ¼" plywood back panel, with the top edge sloped at the same angle as the line between the side panel tops. Attach the back panel to the cabinet with 1" wire nails.

15 Position the small cabinet so the taller side panel is flush against the main cabinet. Align the face of the small cabinet with the face of the main cabinet, then check with a level, and shim if necessary. Connect the cabinets by drilling pilot holes, and driving 1¼" screws through the side panels.

(continued next page)

If corners are open at top and bottom of stairs, attach nailing strips to the understairs cover and cabinet sides, then cut 1/2" plywood panels to fit the space, and attach them to the nailing strips with 1" screws.

16 Measure and cut 1 × 3 bottom rails for the cabinets. Also cut a long, diagonal rail to fit along the edge of the understairs cover. Miter the ends of the diagonal rail to fit against the floor and the side wall, and miter the longer bottom rail to form a clean joint with the diagonal rail. Test-fit the rails, then attach them with glue and 2" finish nails driven through pilot holes.

17 Measure and cut 1 × 3 rails to cover the edges of the connecting shelf and the countertop. Miter the end of the countertop rail that joins the long, diagonal rail. Attach the shelf and countertop rails flush with the countertop and shelf surfaces, using glue and 2" nails driven through pilot holes.

18 Measure and cut 1 × 2 stiles for the front edges of the cabinets. Attach the stiles, flush with the edges of the cabinet sides, using glue and 2" nails driven through pilot holes.

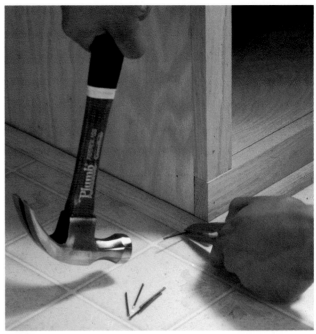

19 Measure and cut 1 × 2 rails to fit between the stiles, so they cover the cabinet shelf edges and are flush with the shelf tops. Attach the rails, using glue and 2" nails driven through pilot holes.

20 Cut base-shoe molding to cover gaps along wall and floor surfaces, mitering the corners. Attach molding, using 1" finish nails. Sand, fill, and finish the understairs center (pages 46 to 49).

21 Attach slide tracks for side-mounted drawer slides, according to the manufacturer's directions.

22 Build, finish, and install drawers (see pages 42 to 45) and drawer hardware. Purchase or build and finish cabinet doors (pages 38 to 41), then hang doors using 3/8" semi-concealed hinges.

Building a Room Divider

A room divider, like a partition wall, separates one large room into two usable spaces, each with its own specific function. But unlike a partition wall, a room divider adds storage space to your home, while letting you retain the open feeling of a larger room.

Room dividers commonly are used to separate a large kitchen/dining area into two different "rooms." Adding a pass-through and overhanging countertop, as in the project shown here, creates a casual dining area.

In the design featured here, the room divider is built in two main sections: the base cabinet with countertop, and the upper shelf unit. The two sections are joined by a floor-to-ceiling plywood framework to create one attractive unit.

A room divider lends itself to personal touches, like mounting a wine rack and stemware racks on the underside of the shelf unit to make a convenient dry bar.

Everything You Need:

Tools: stepladder, pencil, level, tape measure, plumb bob, framing square, router with 3/4" straight bit, circular saw or table saw, handscrew clamps, bar clamps, drill and bits, screwdriver, hammer, nail set, putty knife.

Materials: wood glue, finish nails (1", 1 1/4", 2"), power-driver screws (1", 1 1/4", 2", 2 1/2", 3"), shims, 3/4" hardwood strips, countertop trim, shelf-edge trim, pin-style shelf supports, finishing materials, door hardware.

An overhanging countertop gives this room divider an added dimension as a convenient dining surface located near the food preparation area of the kitchen. The cabinets on the kitchen side of the room divider also provide accessible storage space for pots, pans, and kitchenware. The open shelves in the upper half of the room divider are ideal for displaying glassware or collectibles.

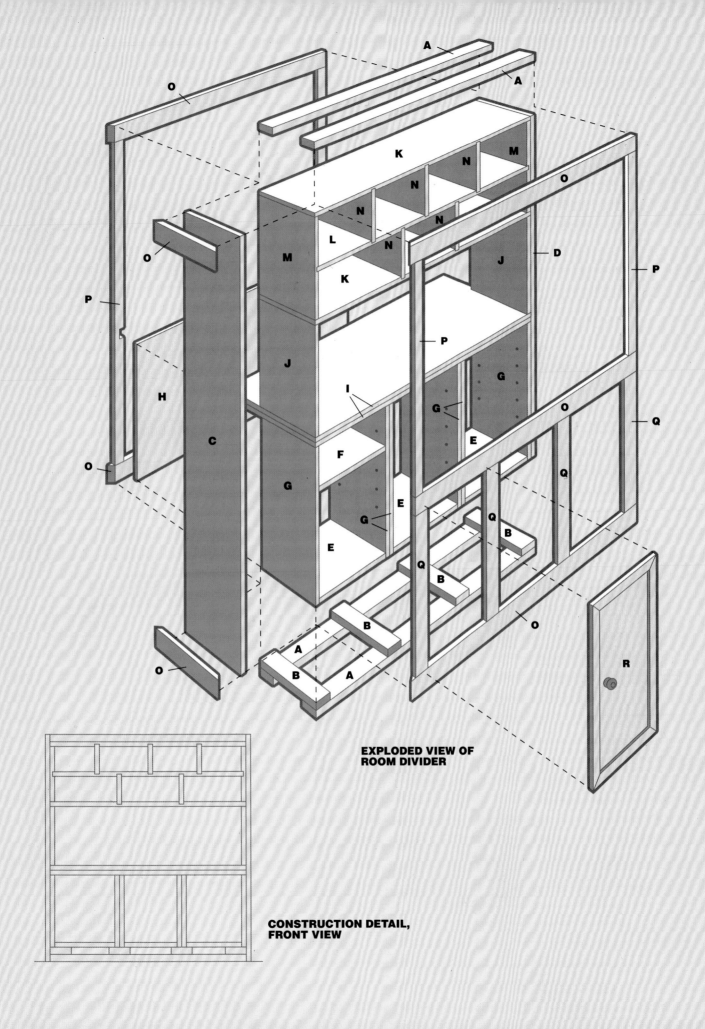

EXPLODED VIEW OF ROOM DIVIDER

CONSTRUCTION DETAIL, FRONT VIEW

Parts List: Room Divider

Key	Part	Material	Pieces	Size	Pieces	Size
		Project as Shown			Your Project	
A	Top and sole plates	2 × 4	4	71 1/4"		
B	Sole plate cross braces	2 × 4	4	15"		
C	Outer end panel	3/4" oak plywood	1	95 1/2" × 15"		
D	Inner end panel	3/4" oak plywood	1	91" × 15"		
E	Base panels	3/4" oak plywood	3	22" × 14 3/4"		
F	Cabinet shelves	3/4" oak plywood	3	21 3/4" × 14 3/4"		
G	Cabinet risers	3/4" oak plywood	6	30" × 14 3/4"		
H	Cabinet back panel	1/4" oak plywood	1	32" × 70"		
I	Countertop panels	3/4" oak plywood	2	70 1/2" × 24"		
J	Shelf unit supports	3/4" oak plywood	2	33" × 15"		
K	Top, bottom shelf panels	3/4" oak plywood	2	70 1/2" × 15"		
L	Center shelf panel	3/4" oak plywood	1	69 3/4" × 15"		
M	Shelf unit sides	3/4" oak plywood	2	25 1/2" × 15"		
N	Shelf unit risers	3/4" oak plywood	5	12 1/2" × 15"		
O	Face frame rails	1 × 4 oak	33 linear ft.			
P	Face frame stiles	1 × 2 oak	26 linear ft.			
Q	Face frame stiles	1 × 3 oak	12 linear ft.			
R	Overlay doors	see pages 38 to 41				

Room Divider Project Details

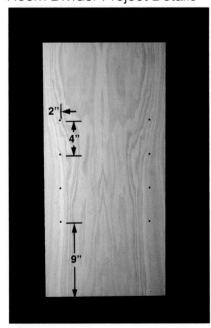

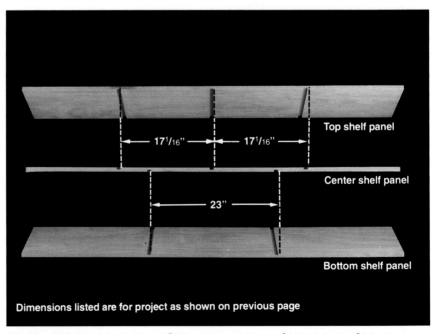

Dimensions listed are for project as shown on previous page

Top shelf panel

17 1/16" 17 1/16"

Center shelf panel

23"

Bottom shelf panel

Cabinet risers, cut from 3/4" plywood, have holes for pin-style shelf supports drilled at 4" intervals, 2" in from edges of each riser face. Holes start 9" from top and bottom.

Shelf-unit panels, cut from 3/4" plywood, have 3/4"-wide by 3/8"-deep dadoes to hold the shelf risers. The center shelf panel is dadoed on both the top and the bottom faces, and the top and bottom shelf panels are dadoed on one face only.

How to Build a Room Divider

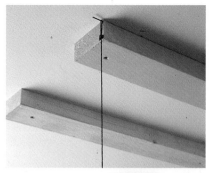

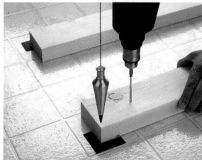

1 Mark the location for the top plates on the ceiling, using a framing square to ensure that lines are perpendicular to the wall. Locate wall studs and ceiling joists in the project area, and install blocking if necessary (page 29).

2 Cut two 2 × 4 top plates and position them against the ceiling, with the outside edges flush against the reference lines. Check to see if plates are level, and install shims if needed. Anchor plates to ceiling joists or blocking, using 3" screws.

3 Cut two 2 × 4 sole plates, and align them directly under the top plates, using a plumb bob as a guide. Check to see if plates are level, shim if needed, then anchor the sole plates to the floor, using 3" screws.

4 Cut and attach 2 × 4 cross braces across the sole plates, using 2¹/2" screws. Position the cross braces at the ends of the sole plates, and below the planned cabinet riser locations.

5 Measure and cut the outer end panel ¹/2" shorter than the floor-to-ceiling height to allow for adjustments. Align end panel with the edges of the 2 × 4 plates, then attach it to the top and sole plates, using 2¹/2" screws driven into counterbored pilot holes.

(continued next page)

6 Measure and cut the inner end panel 1/2" shorter than the distance between the top plate and sole plate cross braces, and slide it in place. Align the panel with the edges of the top plate and sole plate cross braces, then attach it to the wall with 2¹/2" screws driven into wall studs or blocking.

7 Measure and cut plywood cabinet risers with holes for shelf supports (see Project Details, page 108). Risers should be 1/4" narrower than end panels, and 1¹/2" shorter than the distance from sole plate cross braces to planned countertop height. Attach a riser to each end panel, flush with the front edge, by driving 1¹/4" screws through counterbored pilot holes.

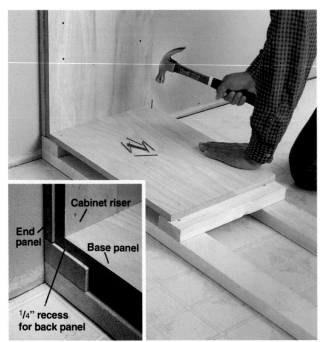

Cabinet riser
End panel
Base panel
1/4" recess for back panel

8 Measure and cut plywood base panels the same width as the risers. Lay one base panel across the sole plate cross braces, butted against the riser at the inner end panel, with the 1/4" recess at the back side (inset). Attach the base panel, using 2" finish nails.

9 Make riser assemblies (for inner riser locations) by joining two risers together, back-to-back, with glue and 1¹/4" finish nails. Set one riser assembly on the cross brace next to the first base panel, and attach it with 2¹/2" screws driven through pilot holes and into the base panel edge.

10 Install the middle base panel, then the second riser assembly, then the last base panel, using the techniques shown in steps 8 to 9.

11 Measure and cut two plywood countertop panels, 24" wide, to fit between the end panels, and set the first panel on the cabinet risers, flush with the front edges of the end panels. Use a framing square to adjust the risers so they are perpendicular to the countertop, then drill pilot holes and drive $2^1/2$" screws through countertop and into risers.

12 Apply glue to the top of the first countertop panel, then set the second countertop panel on the first panel. Clamp the panels together, then join them by driving 1" screws up through the underside of the first panel.

13 Measure and cut a $1/4$" oak plywood back panel to fit into the recess created by the back edges of the risers and base panels (see step 8). Set the back panel into the recess, then attach it to the cabinet risers and base panels, using 1" wire nails driven at 8" intervals.

(continued next page)

Top shelf panel

Center shelf panel

14 Measure and cut plywood shelf panels for the upper shelf unit, then cut 3/4"-wide, 3/8"-deep dadoes at shelf riser locations (see Project Details, page 108). **TIP:** "Gang-cut" dadoes to speed up your work: mark locations for dado cuts on panels, then clamp them together so dado marks align.

15 Measure and cut plywood shelf unit sides. Make a 3/4"-wide, 3/8"-deep dado in each side, where the center shelf panel will fit.

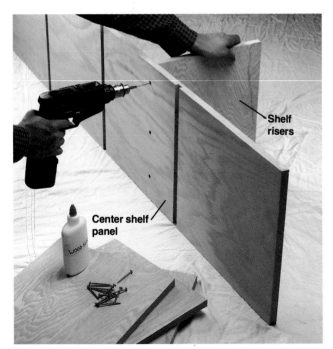

Shelf risers

Center shelf panel

16 Measure and cut plywood shelf unit risers the same width as the center shelf. Stand the center shelf panel on its side, then glue the shelf risers into dadoes. Reinforce the joints with 2" screws driven into counterbored pilot holes.

Bottom shelf panel

17 Assemble the remaining pieces of the upper shelf unit, using glue and 2" screws driven into counterbored pilot holes. Attach side panels to center shelf, then attach top and bottom shelf panels to side panel and shelf risers. Make sure diagonal measurements of shelf unit are equal (if not, adjust unit as needed until it is square).

18 Measure and cut plywood shelf unit supports. Supports should be tall enough to leave a gap of about 1" beneath the top plates when the shelf unit is mounted on their top edges. Attach the shelf unit supports to the inner and outer end panels, using glue and 1¹/4" finish nails.

19 With a helper, lift the shelf unit onto the tops of the shelf unit supports. There should be a gap of about 1" between the shelf unit and the top plates.

20 Align the edges of the upper shelf unit with the edges of the end panels. Attach the shelf unit by driving 1¹/4" finish nails through the side panels and into the end panels. Space nails 4" apart, along outer edges of shelf unit.

21 Set a 2 × 4 brace between the countertop and the shelf unit, then measure and cut 1 × 4 top and bottom rails for the face frames. Miter the corner joints at the edges of the outer end panel, and butt the trim against the wall at the inner end panel. Drill pilot holes, and attach rails with glue and 2" finish nails driven into panels and framing members.

(continued next page)

22 Measure and cut 1 × 4 countertop rail to reach from the wall to the outside edge of the outer end panel, on the front side of the room divider. Attach the rail to the edge of the countertop, using glue and 2" finish nails driven through pilot holes.

23 Measure and cut 1 × 2 face frame stiles to fit between the bottom rail and the top rail at the back of the room divider. Make a $3/4$" × $1 1/2$" notch in each stile, where the edge of the countertop will fit. Attach the stiles to the end panels, using glue and 2" finish nails driven through pilot holes.

24 Measure and cut 1 × 2 stiles to fit between the countertop rail and the top rail at the front of the room divider. Position stiles over the edges of the end panel, and attach with glue and 2" finish nails driven through pilot holes.

25 Cover the countertop overhang with ornamental trim molding mitered at a 45° angle at corner joints. Attach with glue and $1 1/2$" finish nails driven through pilot holes.

26 Measure and cut 1 × 3 stiles to fit between the bottom rail and the countertop rail on the back side of the room divider. Position end stiles flush with the outside faces of the end panels, and center the interior stiles over the riser assemblies. Attach with glue and 2" finish nails driven through pilot holes.

27 Attach ³/₄" shelf-edge strips to all exposed edges of the upper shelf unit, using glue and 1" finish nails driven through pilot holes. Cut horizontal strips the full length of the shelf unit, then add vertical strips between the horizontal strips.

28 Cut adjustable shelves for the cabinets, attach shelf-edge trim if desired, then install shelves, using pin-style shelf supports (pages 36 to 37).

29 Cover gaps at ceiling with cove molding, and along floor and wall with base shoe molding. Fill holes, sand, then apply finish (pages 46 to 49). Build, finish, and hang overlay cabinet doors (pages 38 to 41). Attach all remaining hardware.

Building an Entertainment Center

This handsome and unique entertainment center provides ample storage for all your home electronics, yet is relatively compact—5 ft. high and less than 7 ft. wide. The three-unit design features a 20"-deep center unit spacious enough to hold a large television set, and two 16"-deep end units ideal for storing stereo speakers, tapes, CDs, and books.

Because the project is built in three units, it is easy to adapt. For example, you might choose to expand the project by building additional end units to occupy a long wall. Or, for a small room you might choose to build only the center unit. You also can change the width of the center unit to match the size of your television set.

Everything You Need:

Tools: tape measure, circular saw, straight-edge guide, pencil, router and bits (3/4" rabbet, 3/4" straight), hammer, drill and bits, power screwdriver, right-angle drill guide, pegboard scraps, miter saw, jig saw, bar clamps, utility knife.

Materials: masking tape, finish nails (11/4", 2"), wood glue, 1" wire nails, shims, power-driver screws (1", 3"), 1/4" oak plywood for top cover, 3/4" wire brads, electrical accessories (pages 50 to 51), drawer and door hardware, finishing materials, base shoe molding.

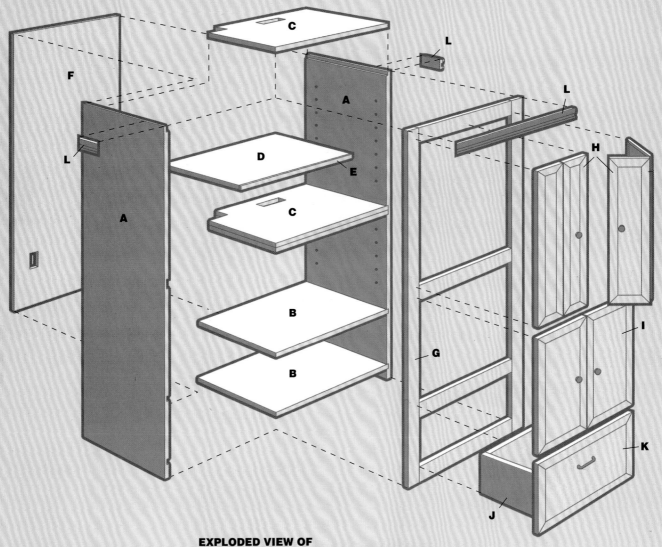

**EXPLODED VIEW OF
ENTERTAINMENT CENTER, CENTER UNIT**

Parts List: Center Unit

		Project as Shown				Your Project	
Key	**Part**	**Material**	**Pieces**	**Size**		**Pieces**	**Size**
A	Side panels	3/4" oak plywood	2	20" × 60"			
B	Bottom panels	3/4" oak plywood	2	20" × 31 1/4"			
C	Permanent shelves	3/4" oak plywood	3	20" × 31 1/4"			
D	Adjustable shelves	3/4" oak plywood	2	19 1/2" × 30 1/4"			
E	Shelf edges	Shelf-edge molding	31 linear ft.				
F	Back panel	1/2" oak plywood	1	32" × 60"			
G	Face frame	1 × 3	23 linear ft.				
H	Folding door panels	1/2" oak plywood	4	6" × 23 1/2"			
I	Overlay doors	pages 38 to 41					
J	Overlay drawer	pages 42 to 45					
K	Drawer face	1/2" oak plywood	1	9" × 27"			
L	Top trim	Ornamental molding	6 linear ft.				

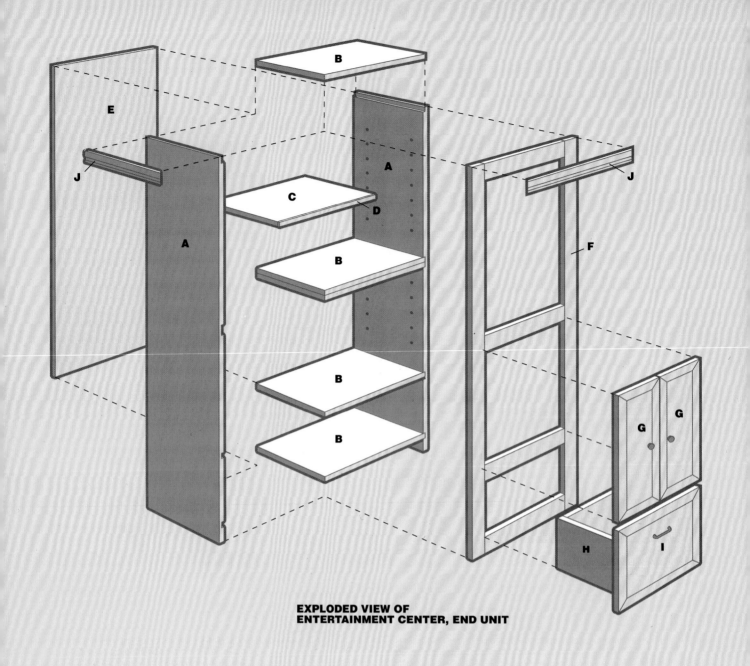

**EXPLODED VIEW OF
ENTERTAINMENT CENTER, END UNIT**

Parts List: For Each End Unit

		Project as Shown			Your Project	
Key	**Part**	**Material**	**Pieces**	**Size**	**Pieces**	**Size**
A	Side panels	3/4" oak plywood	2	16" × 60"		
B	Fixed shelves	3/4" oak plywood	5	16" × 23¹/4"		
C	Adjustable shelves	3/4" oak plywood	2	15¹/2" × 22¹/4"		
D	Shelf-edges	Shelf-edge molding	2	22¹/4"		
E	Back panel	1/2" oak plywood	1	24" × 60"		
F	Face frame	1 × 3	20 linear ft.			
G	Overlay doors		pages 38 to 41			
H	Overlay drawer		pages 42 to 45			
I	Drawer face	1/2" oak plywood	1	9" × 22"		
J	Top trim	Ornamental molding	3 linear ft.			

Entertainment Center Project Details

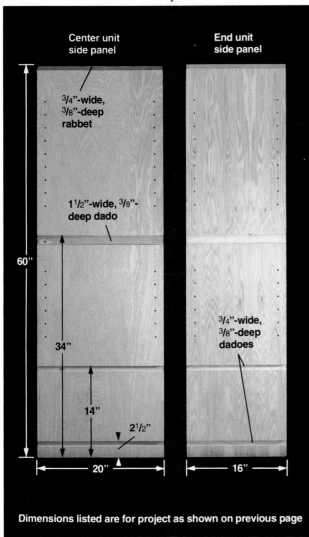

Center unit side panel

End unit side panel

3/4"-wide, 3/8"-deep rabbet

1 1/2"-wide, 3/8"-deep dado

3/4"-wide, 3/8"-deep dadoes

60"

34"

14"

2 1/2"

20"

16"

Dimensions listed are for project as shown on previous page

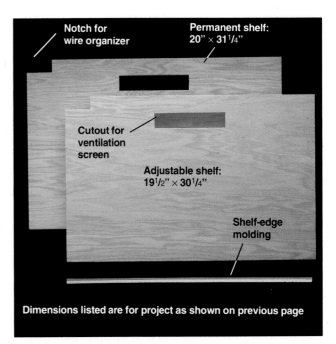

Notch for wire organizer

Permanent shelf: 20" × 31 1/4"

Cutout for ventilation screen

Adjustable shelf: 19 1/2" × 30 1/4"

Shelf-edge molding

Dimensions listed are for project as shown on previous page

Center unit shelves (above) made from 3/4" plywood have notches cut in the back corner to accommodate a vertical wire organizer track, and cutouts sized to hold ventilation screens. Adjustable shelves are faced with shelf-edge molding.

Side panels (left) for center unit and end unit are made from 3/4" plywood, and differ only in width. Dadoes and rabbets will hold the top panel, bottom panel, and permanent shelves. Parallel rows of peg holes, drilled 2" from front and back edges and beginning 4 1/2" above permanent shelves, will hold pin-style supports for the adjustable shelves.

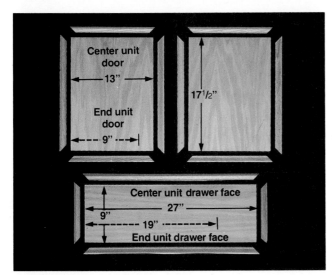

Center unit door
13"

17 1/2"

End unit door
9"

Center unit drawer face
27"

9"

19"

End unit drawer face

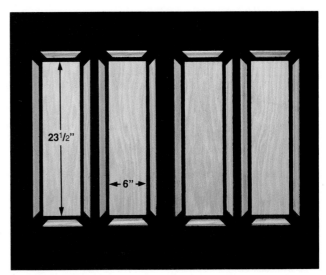

23 1/2"

6"

Drawer faces & overlay doors are built with 1/2" plywood framed with mitered door-edge molding. Doors and drawers for end units are the same height as those for the center unit, but are not as wide.

Folding doors for center unit are made of 1/2" plywood panels, framed on all sides by mitered door-edge molding. Two butt hinges join each pair of framed panels.

How to Build an Entertainment Center

1 Remove baseboards and other moldings, then mark the planned location of the entertainment center on the floor, using masking tape. **NOTE:** Back panel of the entertainment center can be cut out to provide access to a wall receptacle located in the project area.

2 Measure and cut ³/4" plywood side panels for the center unit, using a circular saw and a straight-edge guide (page 23).

3 Cut rabbets and dadoes (page 33) in the side panels at the locations shown in the Project Details (page 119), using a router and two straight-edge guides.

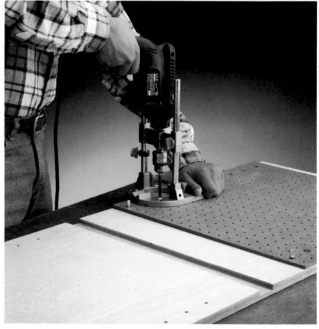

4 Drill two vertical rows of ¹/4" holes along the inside face of each side panel to hold pin-style shelf supports. Use a right-angle drill guide, and a pegboard scrap as a template to ensure that holes are aligned correctly (page 37). Holes should be drilled 2" from the edges of the panels.

5 Measure and cut 3/4" plywood permanent shelves and adjustable shelves. Use a jig saw to cut corner notches where wire organizer will fit, and to make cutouts for ventilation screens (see Project Details, page 119).

6 Join two of the notched permanent shelves together with glue and 1¼" finish nails to form one double-layer shelf for the middle of the center unit.

7 Measure and cut shelf-edge molding to cover the exposed front edges of the adjustable shelves. Glue and clamp the molding to the shelves, then drill pilot holes and drive 1¼" finish nails through the molding and into the shelves.

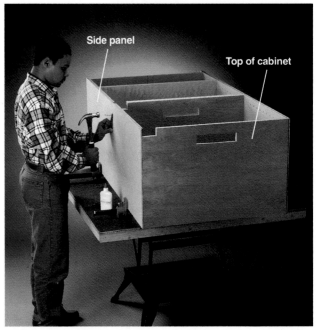

8 Measure and cut 3/4" plywood bottom panels, then attach the track for a center-mounted drawer slide at the center of one of the bottom panels (pages 42 to 45).

9 Glue and clamp the bottom panels and permanent shelves between the side panels to form dado and rabbet joints. Reinforce each joint with 2" finish nails driven 4" to 6" apart.

(continued next page)

 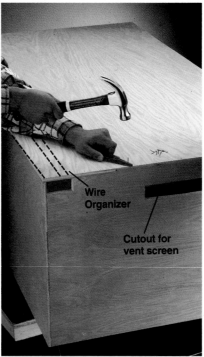 

10 Measure and cut ¹/₂" plywood back panel, then tack a 30" wire organizer track 1" from the edge of the panel, along the side where the notches will be located.

11 Position the back panel over the back of the center unit so edges are flush. Attach it by driving wire nails every 4" into the shelves and side panels.

12 If cabinet will cover a wall receptacle, make a cutout in the back panel, slightly larger than the coverplate, to provide access to the receptacle.

13 Position the center unit against the wall inside the floor outline. Check with a level, and shim under the sides of the center unit, if necessary, until it is level and plumb. Score shims with a utility knife, and snap off the excess.

14 Measure, cut, and prepare side panels, permanent shelves, and back panel for each end unit (see Project Details, page 119), then assemble the pieces, following steps 2 to 9.

15 Position the end units next to the center unit. If necessary, shim under the side panels to align the tops of the end units with the center unit.

16 Join each end unit to the center unit by drilling counterbored pilot holes and driving 1" screws through the side panels and into the center unit.

17 Anchor the center unit and end units to the wall by drilling counterbored pilot holes and driving 3" screws through the back panels and into the wall at stud locations.

18 Measure and cut 1 × 3 vertical face frame stiles and attach them to the center unit and end units, using glue and finish nails driven through pilot holes. Edges of stiles should be flush with outside edges of the side panels.

(continued next page)

19 Cut 1 × 3 horizontal face frame rails to fit between the stiles, along the edges of the permanent shelves and bottom panels. Attach them with glue and 2" finish nails, so upper edges of the rails are flush with the top surfaces of the shelves and bottom panels. Anchor the rails to the stiles by drilling pilot holes and driving 2" finish nails diagonally through the rails and into the stiles (inset).

20 Lay a sheet of 1/4" oak plywood on the entertainment center, and outline the top of the entertainment center onto the plywood. Also mark cutouts for the wire organizer notch and ventilation screen. Cut the plywood along the marked lines, using a jig saw, then attach it to the top of the entertainment center with 3/4" wire brads.

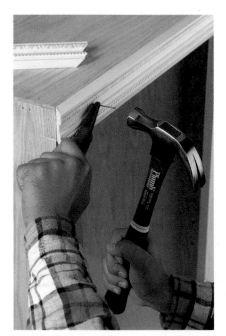

21 Trim the top of the entertainment center with mitered ornamental molding to cover the exposed edges of the plywood. Attach the moldings by drilling pilot holes and driving 1 1/4" finish nails into the top rails and side panels.

22 Cover gaps along the wall and floor with base shoe molding, attached with 1" finish nails driven through pilot holes.

23 Fill and plug the nail and screw holes, then sand and finish the entertainment center (pages 46 to 49).

24 Insert ventilation screens into the cutouts in the shelf panels, then attach an electrical outlet strip to the back panel on the center cabinet, just above the double-layer middle shelf.

25 If you need to run wires between units, cut holes through side panels, using a hole saw or forstner bit, and install grommets.

26 Build folding overlay doors for center unit by framing two pairs of 1/2" plywood panels with door-edge molding (see Project Details, page 119). Finish doors to match entertainment center, then join each pair with butt hinges attached to backs of panels.

27 Mount the folding doors to the center unit face frame with semi-concealed hinges (pages 38 to 41).

28 Build, finish, and install remaining overlay doors (pages 38 to 41) and drawers (pages 42 to 45) for the center unit and end unit. (**NOTE:** The drawer design for this project varies slightly from standard design by using framed plywood panels, not solid hardwood, for the drawer faces.) Attach drawer pulls and doorknobs.

INDEX